T

SHARK
BELIEF

SUCCESS CODE

How to Hack the Six Principles
Needed to
Achieve Excellence

ERNIE AYON

THE SHARK BELIEF SUCCESS CODE
© **March 2016**
By ERNIE AYON

For information visit www.sharkbelief.com

Book Cover design by Pulp Art

Zaden Publishing

ISBN 978-0-9972191-1-1

First Edition: March 2016

To Jeanette,

Your encouragement and unwavering support

made all the difference.

This was possible because of you.

…You too little Z.

Contents

INTRODUCTION

The Formula for Success

Is there a formula for success? That is the question I sought to answer over 15 years ago. It is this elusive formula for success that I have intensely pursued for more than a decade alongside my many endeavors in business and personal development. I wondered if there was a master key or secret that anyone could use to succeed at anything they pursued? We all dream of success in one form or another and we all have our own definitions of what success is. The popular definitions of success are typically associated with material wealth and financial abundance or with prestige, fame and power. What is it that separates those few that seem to find success so easily from the multitudes that labor for a lifetime and yet never achieve their dreams and goals?

Early in my college experience, I read a couple of books that sparked my interest into the subject of success. These two books were *Rich Dad Poor Dad*, by Robert Kiyosaki, and a biography of John D.

Rockefeller. As I read the stories of men who had become incredibly wealthy and successful in business, I began to wonder if they knew secrets that the average person did not possess. I wondered if there was a formula or a key to success that could be applied by anyone. I was convinced there was, so the question became *"What is the formula for success?"* and I began my quest.

I researched the subject of success while also learning about a wide array of topics such as real estate investing, stock trading, and entrepreneurship. I started business and gained some real experience and further insight into what it took to be successful. It was while learning about these various industries that I began to see more and more examples of ultra-successful individuals and I studied them to look for clues that would reveal how they had become so successful. I increased my level of reading and dove into books like *Think and Grow Rich* and anything on personal development. I read biographies of successful businessmen and women, politicians and star athletes. I attended seminars and listened to recordings from speakers such as Les Brown and Tony Robbins. I began associating with "like-minded people" and always examined my own personal successes and failures to look for clues.

Suddenly, I began to see it. The result of reading hundreds of books, listening to thousands of hours of audio and attending count-less seminars, all while asking, *"what is the formula for success?"*, is that a pattern emerged and it would eventually become the SHARK Belief Success Code. I noticed similar echoes coming from those that had achieved massive success. After reading hundreds of books, I realized that they were all basically saying the same thing. I summarized the main ideas and found that it could all be reduced to fit into six core categories. These were the common denominators for success. This was the code!

Some claim that the key to success is passion; others say it's hard work and relationships and many more will tell you that it's all in your mind. What I realized was that there is no single key to success. No magic bullet can guarantee the attainment of all my desires. However, as I had suspected, there is a formula to success and success in anything requires the same common elements.

It was my 15-year pursuit that led me to identify these core elements. It was the result of persistent learning and questioning. It was the outcome of my personal successes as well as my failures. I had a revelation that gave me insight into the six core elements and I ultimately organized them to form what is now the SHARK Belief Success Code. I tested this formula and began to share it with others. The more I did, the stronger my convictions became that I had successfully simplified all of the teachings and my years of experience into six simple and easy to understand principles that could be tailored for anyone and for any goal. I hesitate to call it a formula because SHARK Belief is so much more than that. It's more than just an equation or recipe that yields the same results each time. Rather, SHARK Belief can more accurately be described as an approach or philosophy for success. This book contains both tactical and philosophical elements that will help you succeed. I will show you why each component is critical to success but I'll also give you practical and easy ways to begin applying them to your own life.

Success is within your reach and is entirely possible for your life! This will serve as your guide and should be referred to often along your journey to success. It's densely packed with practical methods that go far beyond just helping you achieve your goal and will also help you grow personally. Applying the principles of SHARK Belief is transformative and you will see changes in many areas of your life. You will start to think differently and you'll find yourself acting in new ways. You'll have a greater sense of confidence and satisfaction. You'll push yourself harder and find yourself reaching bigger goals. Luckily, you don't need to spend 15 years searching for the formula to success. You have the code and can approach your goals much more effectively and see results much sooner. While the methods and tactics for implementing SHARK Belief may change over the years, the essence of the six core elements will always be required for success.

You have here a simplified, yet complete outline on the rules for success. You are holding the fruits of lessons from both successes and failures. You are approaching a launching pad from which you can start much higher and rise much faster than I did. There is no need for you to start from the bottom. As Sir Isaac Newton so aptly put it, "If I have seen further, it is by standing on the shoulders of Giants." You too can stand on the shoulders of Giants. My hope is that you will embrace these teachings and go on to accomplish great things in your life, perhaps even surprising yourself. My goal is that you will SHARK Belief your life!

P.S. – This book is NOT about sharks! It doesn't get into the magic of shark-fin soup, or shark's blood or shark teeth or even about behaving like a shark. As amazing as those creatures are, this book has nothing to do with the study sharks for success. Although I do explain the reason for the hammerhead shark symbol, you'll soon understand why it's called SHARK Belief.

CHAPTER ONE

The New Definition of Success

Do you want success in life? Of course you do. Every person does, but unfortunately it's only a small percentage that are actually willing to do what it takes to be successful. If you're like me, then you know you are and have always been a little different from most people. You have big dreams. You're ambitious and motivated. You're interested in different things than your family and enjoy learning about personal development and success. Perhaps other see you as being a bit weird. You want to do more with your life and you won't settle for average. You want to create and innovate and ultimately, you want to succeed. This book is for you.

The SHARK Belief success code is primarily directed at entrepreneurs and business professionals. I teach from this viewpoint because it is the path that I took - the path leading to my discovery of the six elements for success. Because that's my personal experience, it's easier for me to teach SHARK Belief within a business context, but it's important to remember that these principles are universal to success in any field. They go far beyond just business success; they can be applied by anyone, to accomplish any goal. It's an incredible framework for mentors and life coaches to use with their clients. It's a powerful approach for personal growth. It works for aspiring authors, for athletes, and for those ready to take their career to the next level. Many of my examples contain familiar business success stories and thoughts from leaders on personal development, but always keep in mind that the SHARK Belief elements are pivotal components for success in any field.

What is Success?

Before we go into the details of the SHARK Belief Success Code, let's take a quick look at "success." What exactly are we striving to achieve? In the introduction, I briefly described my quest to discover the formula for success. I wanted to learn it because I wanted business and financial success for my own life. But everyone's life is different. Everyone's goals are different. If "success" is what we want then let's start with the following question: "What is success?" It sounds like a simple question with an obvious answer, but think about it. Is success some finite destination? Is success having fame and fortune? I've heard that success is a journey and not a destination. Some people say success is the freedom of choice. It's about being able to do what you want, when you want, and with whom you want. That all sounds pretty good to me but is that what success really means?

Do a search for images of "successful people" and you'll see plenty of results showing young, attractive, business professionals wearing expensive suits and standing by luxury cars. You'll also find images of business tycoons like Arianna Huffington and Jeff Bezos.

You'll see images of star athletes and famous actors. No doubt these individuals have all been very successful in their fields but the truth is, you don't need to reach those levels to be considered successful. There are millions of successful individuals that you will never hear about. They'll probably never appear on the cover of Fortune Magazine or give an acceptance speech at the Academy Awards, but you can bet that they are out there and they are reaching new levels of success every day. It's easy to compare ourselves to the rich and famous and begin to believe that we too should be achieving those levels of success or we'll be considered a failure. Success can mean so much more for your life and is well within your reach.

What do successful people look like?

Close your eyes and imagine a successful person. What is the first image that comes to your mind? Is it someone famous? A business mogul perhaps? Most people will describe a good-looking person wearing expensive clothes, driving a nice car, and having achieved wealth, fame, and power. They come from wealthy families and go to Ivy League schools after being raised by loving parents in upper-middle class suburbia. Most people would probably describe a successful person this way because the media defines success based on money and material possessions. There is nothing wrong with being wealthy, but money isn't the only measure of success. Popular media has conditioned us to think of successful people this way. We've been taught that this is the American Dream.

The truth is that there is no standard description of what a successful person looks like. Success is not defined by what you wear or drive and it's certainly not dependent on where you grew up or what your parents did for a living. If I took you to an airport and asked you to pick out the successful from the unsuccessful, you wouldn't be able to do it. Success doesn't care what you look like, whether you're male or female or even about the color of your skin. Success doesn't care what neighborhood you grew up in or how popular you were in school. There is no success gene and people are not born with a God-given ability to become successful & wealthy. Rather, people achieve success because of who they are and who they have become. The underlying theme of SHARK Belief is about "becoming." It's about personal development and it's about making progress. I will teach you about the essential elements and the traits necessary for success, but more importantly, I will show you how to apply them to become the person who attracts the success you desire.

This is What a Successful Person Looks Like

Here is a brief snapshot of what a successful person looks like. A successful person sets goals and maintains a to-do list while the unsuccessful person is unfocused and easily distracted. A successful person talks about their ideas and shares useful information with others, while the unsuccessful person likes to talk about other people and regularly shares criticism. A successful person makes time for personal development by reading books and listening to audio that will help them grow as an individual. The unsuccessful person prefers to watch a lot of TV or spend countless hours playing video games. The successful person is not afraid to fail and always learns from their mistakes rather than blaming others for their failures. The successful person wants others to succeed and compliments others rather than feeling threatened by someone else's success. A successful person seeks to build positive relationships with others and learns from those that have gone before them rather than trying to look like they know it all. A successful person is confident enough to show real humility and gratitude instead of attempting to come across as already being successful. A successful person hustles and works hard at developing new skills and good habits. They have patience and they persist because they understand that success doesn't come easy, so they are willing to put in the time necessary to achieve results.

You see, a successful person is defined by how they live and who they are rather than what they own. The thing that separates the successful and the unsuccessful is what takes place inside their head and it's not limited by genetics or the neighborhood they grew up in. I understand that many people live in communities surrounded by poverty, drugs, and violence. I grew up in such an environment and saw more than my fair share of these things. But I have also realized that in spite of all these external things, anyone can achieve success if they want it bad enough and are willing to do what's necessary to transform who they are.

The New Definition of Success

So then, what is success? Success will mean different things to you at different times of your life, but let me give you the short answer: success is simply accomplishing a personal goal.

For some, success means building a profitable business. For others, it means crossing the finish line in a marathon. Success can mean learning to speak a new language fluently, earning your college degree or writing your first book. For our purposes here, I primarily refer to success in terms of attaining a particular goal, but success can also be a process or ongoing lifestyle. For example, success could be making progress towards a goal and feeling happy about having the freedom and time to do so. Success could mean enjoying the process of learning new skills or training for a race. Being successful does not mean you have to celebrate a major accomplishment every day, or even every month. I used to obsess over my 5-year goals and would have feelings of failure at the end of every year because I felt like I hadn't accomplished the huge goals that I had set for myself. In reality, I was being successful and was growing a lot while accomplishing a bunch of little goals along my journey. It was a change in perspective that led me to redefine what success really means. This is the new definition: Success is both a destination and a journey at the same time.

One aspect of success is event-focused while another is process oriented. You have to live successfully but you also need to succeed in attaining your goals along the way. It's how we measure progress and determine the next steps to take. Take a hunter for example. The prize is to get the big game. However, any hunter will tell you the thrill of the hunt is just as much fun. It's the pursuit that makes it exciting but that effort must eventually culminate into a successful hunt. Viewing success in this light also leads to a more fulfilling life. When you see that you're making progress toward smaller goals while simultaneously keeping the bigger dream alive, you learn to really enjoy the journey along the way. When I say that SHARK Belief will help you be successful, I'm referring to success in terms of who you are and not so much what you do or own. Success reveals itself in all areas of our lives including our health, relationships, finances, and spiritual pursuits.

The best parts of success are the intangible rewards. We all want nice things and greater financial abundance. It's wonderful to have the means to buy new cars and go on exotic vacations. It's an amazing experience when you cross the finish line or stand on the podium as you receive your degree. But the rewards of success are more than just the trophies or a sheet of paper with your name on it. It's about the challenges that you overcame along the way. It's the new skills and knowledge you had to acquire in your pursuit. It's the relationships you made. It's your newfound self-confidence and wisdom. Your life experiences make success rewarding. It's who you have become in the process of your pursuits that will ultimately make you a successful and fulfilled person.

Like that old proverb says, the journey is the reward. But it's also important to remember that any good journey also needs a destination! That is why I say success has two key elements: the goal and the transformation process. Les Brown shared some insights that I remind myself of regularly. He said, "You don't get in life what you want. You get in life what you are." Who we are is a result of our beliefs, our skills, our habits, our knowledge and our experiences. Personal development is a life-long pursuit broken up into short sprints toward smaller goals. Jim Rohn put it perfectly when he said, "Your level of success will seldom exceed your level of personal development." He also said that success was not something to be pursued but rather something to be attracted. We attract the success we want by becoming the person we need to be. Success is more than just "doing" the right things or "knowing" the right people. It's a product of who you are. That is the essence of the SHARK Belief Success Code. It is about becoming. It is about transforming you. You must become the person that attracts the level of success you want to achieve. I will show you how to become that person by teaching you the six elements of SHARK Belief and how you can apply them as your formula for success.

They Don't Teach Success in School

I've always wondered why public schools don't teach students about the critical life areas before they head out into the real world. In general, the traditional education system today neglects some key learning points that leave most students completely lost when it comes to succeeding in life. Don't get me wrong; I am not anti-school or anti-education. As a matter of fact, I love learning and have given a few colleges and universities A LOT of money over the years for two degrees and various additional classes that I choose to take for my own personal interests. There is an entire chapter in this book dedicated to Knowledge as an essential ingredient for success and I believe schools and early education play a key role in the progress of any society. However, the things I've learned about success and personal development—those things that have made the most difference in my life—I had to learn outside of the traditional educational system. I had to discover and read personal development books. I've paid for and attended many seminars and workshops on success. Yes, I've gone to those crazy and exciting Tony Robbins events! I have been fortunate to meet people that have had a profound influence on my life. Still, I didn't learn any of these things growing up or while in school, and neither did most of my friends and family.

When it comes to basic education in our public schools, I'm disappointed at how little emphasis is placed on learning critical life skills such as effective goal setting and building successful habits. I rarely see classes on the value of personal networking, finding mentors, or developing leadership ability. Schools are good at getting students to learn some vital skills such as reading, writing, and arithmetic, but beyond that, education is overly focused on getting students to memorize facts and pass standardized tests. Sure, those facts have done wonders for helping me win at trivia games but it's done absolutely nothing for personal development or for reaching high levels of success in life!

Most schools don't teach you that the real world pays you for your skills and the value you provide to others. Only now are they starting to emphasize building your personal reputation and brand image. They don't like to say that companies won't hire you just because of where you went to school or simply because you earned a degree. Most schools don't teach that there are many more ways to earn an income apart from getting a traditional job. Freelancing, building startups, entrepreneurship, sales, and income from royalties and investments are rarely mentioned.

My point is not to rant against the school system or accuse parents of failing to teach their children critical life skills. Rather I want to highlight the fact that we all need to be taught the fundamental elements necessary for achieving anything worthwhile with our lives. These are typically not intuitive or passed down from our parents. Just look at the Forbes 400 list and you'll find the majority of the billionaires on that list are first-generation rich. Without someone teaching us how to succeed, we're left to stumble through life trying to figure it out along the way. Is it any wonder the vast majority of our society is unhappy at work, heavily in debt and has very little money saved for retirement? Too many people view success only as it's been glamorized in the media and have set false expectations for themselves. There is an over-emphasis on the "BLING" and very little is said about the process. Too often, we only see the outcomes of success and never see the effort that made it possible. We have lost sight of the hustle, the grit and the utter level of perseverance that is required to succeed at anything.

I'm afraid that too many people have settled and are no longer dreaming big, but are now just trying to get by. They tried and failed and were somehow convinced that success is life is no longer possible for them. I will show you why failure is not the end and that regardless of your current place in life, you can still achieve anything you want. It has never been easier. I would love to see schools teaching our youth how to succeed at anything. It would be amazing to take a class that teaches what success really is and how to accomplishing anything. We need to be taught how to construct a personal plan to reach any target.

That is the gap this book aims to fill. Not just for our youth, but for anyone who's ever wanted to achieve more with their life. The elements discussed within the SHARK Belief Success Code are those missing pieces to the puzzle that can take the potential within every person and turn it into a life of satisfaction, contribution, and world-changing achievement. The world as we know it is changing fast and will continue to do so, but the fundamentals for achieving success are still the same.

My vision is to see one million people learn the principles taught in SHARK Belief. How different would your life be if you had the formula to reach any goal you wanted? How much more would our world change if one million people had that formula and used it to reach their full potential? What if society embraced the new definition of success? Imagine the world-changing inventions that could be created, the books that would be written, the new technologies and discoveries we would see! Perhaps that is a little too grandiose for now, so I'll start with changing my immediate community.

If you're reading this, then you have already discovered your desire for personal growth and the need for improvement. You want more success and you're ready to learn how to get there. Success means something different for everyone, but you already have an idea of what that means for you. My aim in teaching you the SHARK Belief Success Code is to show you how to realize your dreams, but I also want you to learn enough that you too can show someone else the way. As the old proverb says, "Give a man a fish and you'll feed him for a day. Teach a man to fish and you'll feed him for a lifetime." SHARK Belief is about teaching you how to fish and helping you take your fishing beyond the small pond you've been stuck in and into the oceans of success awaiting those that would dare to dream big.

CHAPTER TWO

An Overview of SHARK Belief

It was the last week of December and I was doing what I always do at this time of the year. I was taking stock of the prior year and reviewing my goals and accomplishments. I had come up short again. "But why!?", I asked myself. I had read the books, attended seminars and was taking bold and consistent action. I had studied success for years now. As the frustration swelled within me, I regained my focus and began to search for answers. I suppose it's the engineer in me that wants to analyze everything, so I started an already familiar process. First, I looked at what had gone right and what worked well. Then I looked for gaps in my approach, finding clues as to what I had missed or failed to do. And then, I saw it.

The more I wrote, the clearer it became. It was as if I had finally put all the puzzle pieces together and could see the entire picture for success. I would like to claim that it was a Eureka moment, but the truth is, that clarity came only because I had already dedicated years of study to the subject. I was already familiar with most of the critical elements. Nevertheless, when I finally saw it, it was entirely clear and obvious to me. It was almost too simple but each time I tested it, I found it to be complete.

I simplified everything I learned over the years and put it into six simple terms that would go on to become SHARK Belief. I compared it to the teachings of all the authors and mentors I had learned from. I challenged it by using the theories of SHARK Belief to analyze the successes of current day achievers such as Arnold Schwarzenegger, Oprah Winfrey, and Elon Musk. I was not let down. The more I looked for it the more I saw it. I would recognize it in every book I read, in every success story I heard, and even in my own life. It was the formula I had been looking for.

The Many 'Secrets' to Success

There is no shortage of people who claim to have the secret to success. Countless books offer secrets on what it takes to be successful and plenty of blogs offer advice on how to do it. You can spend a fortune going to seminars and receiving coaching from those who claim to have the secrets to making you successful. There is an infinite supply of good tips and advice out there. However, it's also this wealth of information that made my quest for the formula so difficult. It was information overload and I had to find a way to separate the wheat from the chaff, as they say.

Many of the books I read contained some real gems, but they were often hidden in hundreds of pages of fluff and heartwarming stories. Other books were completely off target and could have saved me time and confusion had they been avoided altogether. The same could be said for many of the workshops I attended. What I found most often, however, is that many of these authors and teachers were partially correct. They presented some great ideas but rarely offered a complete picture.

For example, if we look at some of the most popular advice on what it takes to be successful, you'll hear the following statements:

- The secret to success is passion.
- Follow your dreams, do what you love, and you'll be successful.
- The secret to success is hard work and persistence. You need to hustle.
- It's all about how you think. Your success depends on your thoughts.
- It's not what you know, but *who* you know that matters.
- You have to be different. If you follow the crowd, you'll end up mediocre.
- You need to be super smart, so read a lot of books and get a good education.

The list is endless and if I begin to add famous quotes regarding the "secrets to success" it will consume the rest of this chapter. My point is that it can quickly become overwhelming and begs the following questions, "Which secret is the right secret?", "If there are so many secrets, is there a REAL secret?" and most importantly, if there is a secret to success, "Whose advice should I follow?"

There are two primary challenges with all the teachings on how to achieve success. The first is what I call the Holy Grail Approach. With it, we are led to believe that there is a single secret to success—that if we just do this one thing, we will achieve everything we desire. Books like *The Secret* for example. The reality is, there is no one-size-fits-all approach or step-by-step how-to that applies to every person and every situation. If there were, it would have been discovered a long time ago and we would all be driving Ferraris and running four-minute miles. However, each person is much too unique and every goal is much too different to be pursued with the same Holy Grail Approach.

The second is what I call the Philosopher's Approach. This is on the opposite end of the spectrum, and is more of an abstract approach. It teaches success from a deeper and broader perspective. It's highly motivational in nature and opens the mind to new ideas and perspectives. The problem, however, is that while the message may inspire you and make you feel good about becoming successful, you're often left wondering where to start or what to do next. The teachings cover many different topics and are usually more theoretical than tactical. This often leads to paralysis by analysis: you begin to believe that before you can start your journey, you need to learn more to find that missing piece of the puzzle. Unfortunately, you never learn it all and the more you learn, the more missing pieces you discover.

The optimal approach lies somewhere in the middle. That is what makes SHARK Belief superior to other "systems for success." The SHARK Belief Success Code takes a holistic approach by simplifying the necessary traits as much as possible and no more. The code contains six core elements that work in harmony so that you can attain the levels of achievement you desire. You'll find that those taking the Holy Grail Approach often deal with just one or two of the elements, while those on the Philosopher's Approach spend more time thinking than acting. In both cases, their results are often subpar. SHARK Belief offers a simple, comprehensive approach to achieving any goal and for reaching any level of success. That is because SHARK Belief is not a step-by-step formula or a single-trick gimmick. Neither is it a get-rich-quick scheme or an abstract manifesto on the theories of success. SHARK Belief is simple and easy to learn, yet it's also complete and holds up to even the biggest of goals. Let's take a quick overview of each of the elements and how they all combine to make SHARK Belief powerfully effective.

An Overview of SHARK Belief

"Ok, so what is this whole SHARK Belief thing already so I can apply it and start reaching my goals?"

Well, I'm glad you asked!

As I've already mentioned, there are six critical elements necessary for success in anything. They are: Skills, Habits, Aim, Relationships, Knowledge, and Beliefs. The first letter of each component is used to create the easy-to-remember phrase SHARK Belief. While each individual element is powerful on its own, SHARK Belief combines all six elements to create a whole far greater than the sum of its parts.

You can describe it as a code, a map, or a formula. To successfully reach any goal, all six primary elements must be understood and applied together. Imagine trying to cook a gourmet dish by following a recipe. Individually, some of the ingredients may not taste all that great. But when mixed together in the right proportions, the result is like magic! What if you left out just one of the ingredients? The dish may still taste okay but it certainly won't be great. Even worse, it might be a total disaster if you were to leave out the salt or sugar. The point is, to reach your full potential in whatever capacity you aim for, you need ALL SIX of the elements working together to give you optimal results. There is a harmonious effect when all are in play and the result is not just 2X or 6X better. It's 10X and even 100X better!

Let's take a quick look at each element.

Skills - When trying to reach any goal, there are certain skills you must develop. Some goals require you to master highly sophisticated skills while others call for a simple understanding of basic techniques. Skill is not the same as talent. Talent describes a natural aptitude while skills are developed and mastered through learning, repetition, and focus. Anyone can become highly skilled, and it has more to do with out-working those around you than it does with being gifted. Having a natural talent definitely helps for some skills, but it is not necessary for most goals or for reaching success. This is especially important if your goals are in the areas of business and entrepreneurship.

Habits – Apart from beliefs, Habits are the key differentiator between those who fail and those who succeed. The successful have habits and routines entirely different from those who are unsuccessful. The majority of your life is shaped by daily and weekly habits and routines that are generally the same day in and day out— often performed subconsciously. The good news is you can create new habits that will give you the momentum to take the actions necessary to achieve your goal.

There is a tremendous amount of power that comes from consistent action. It is the compounding effect of routines that give them so much impact. Just like exercise, one day at the gym will not make much of a difference, but the cumulative effect of a good exercise routine is nothing short of amazing as it transforms the body. You must also identify and replace those habits holding you back. We are often blind to the repeated actions that self-sabotage our success. Since habits drive much of our behavior, achieving success in any goal will require you to establish habits and routines that will move you toward your aim. You can achieve the extraordinary by doing the ordinary, consistently!

Aim – Simply put, this is the goal you are trying to achieve; the end result you're after. This is your purpose, your target, or your desire. You must have a definite chief aim. Success begins with first defining exactly what you want to accomplish so that your energy is focused and your thoughts and actions are organized. This is especially critical for entrepreneurs as we're prone to want to chase after many things at once. Your aim will help you determine how to implement the rest of the SHARK Belief formula. This is the cornerstone to achieving your goal. Without a defined target, you will never know when you've been successful.

Relationships – We've all heard the saying "it's not what you know but who you know." To be clear, *what* you know actually matters a lot. However, your relationships are critical to success in any field. Relationships will shape your environment, your thinking, and ultimately whether or not you're successful in reaching your aim. Your network, your friends and family, acquaintances, mentors, coaches and teachers. Even your rivals and competitors, your neighbors and the strangers around you work together to create your environment. They reflect who you are or who you will become. Always remember, you will eventually become like those you associate with. Some people will propel you forward while others can hold you back. Relationships in the context of SHARK Belief is about seeking those who will help you reach your goal while avoiding those who will hold you back.

Knowledge - Knowledge truly is power. Yet knowledge is only potential power until you put it into action. Be careful:

knowledge is not the same as information. We have vast amounts of information at our fingertips, but we have to be particular about what we take in and how we synthesize it for our use. What you know matters and what you don't know may be preventing you from reaching your goal. Continually learn, seek wisdom and guidance, and identify the specific information you need to reach your goal. The process of gaining knowledge never ends so don't wait until you feel like you know enough to begin. Take action and learn along the way. It is by doing that we identify the next piece of knowledge to seek. As you'll see later, all of the six elements work in harmony and you'll gain the knowledge you need through meeting others, defining your goal, and developing your skills.

Beliefs – Your mindset is the secret sauce that brings the entire formula together. Your thinking, your whys, your motivation, your values, your faith, and even your limiting self-doubts and fears will all collaborate to influence your level of success. The mind is more powerful than most people realize. You can leverage and program your subconscious mind to help you achieve success. Your thoughts and belief system form your character and drive your actions, and it is your thoughts and beliefs that will mold your realities and shape your destiny. Beliefs will change your world!

You must believe that reaching your aim is not only possible, but that you will actually be successful in reaching it. This goes beyond just visualization and the law of attraction. Beliefs include your perspectives on success and failure, your limiting self-doubts and fears, your self-confidence and your overall mindset. You must learn to control and influence both the conscious and subconscious levels of your mind.

SHARK Belief breaks down all the main ideas of success philosophy into these simple and easy to understand concepts. As you learn more about them, you'll begin to recognize the six elements in just about every seminar, book, or audio program you come across. They may go by different names, but in the end they will be found in one form or another. For example, Aim is commonly referred to as goals or life purpose. Habits are often called routines, rituals, and patterns.

The biggest and most important element in the group is Beliefs. Depending on your goal, it may require addressing some deep-rooted beliefs that you have about success and failure. Also, negative beliefs about yourself may have been reinforced through the years and are holding you back. For most of us, the area of beliefs will be the hardest to recognize and change. However, once changed, beliefs will completely change who you are and ultimately change the world you live in. I will share some essential beliefs you should adopt to improve your success. I will also show you how you can change your beliefs with easy to follow techniques.

SHARK Belief is the result of years of practicing, learning, and researching the field of personal development and success. This is the book I wish I had read years ago! Many others will claim to have the "key" to success or the "secret." While they may identify some vital laws or ideas, I have found that they often leave out several of the key elements I describe and you end up getting only half of the advice. That's okay if you are already aware of the other aspects and just want to go deeper into one particular topic. But if you're just getting started, then understanding the six elements of the SHARK Belief Success Code is the first step. If you have tried other methods but just can't seem to get a breakthrough, chances are you have missed one of the six elements, but you are probably much closer to success than you realize. One essential ingredient may be all that's missing.

A Quick Note on the Hammerhead Shark

As you may have noticed, the logo for SHARK Belief contains a shark. That's pretty obvious but more specifically, the logo must always be a *hammerhead* shark. Not just any shark. Not a great white shark or a blue shark or a sand tiger shark, but a hammerhead shark! I'm often asked why I prefer the hammerhead to other types of sharks. It's quite straightforward. When looking at the silhouette of the hammerhead, you know what it is. You don't wonder if it's a fish, or a whale, or a dolphin. It clearly is a shark, and not just any shark, but a hammerhead!

It's one of the most unique and beautiful sharks in the world. The distinctive, flat head makes for a unique appearance. It can be found in every ocean in the world and comes in a variety of sizes and colors, and even the shape of their heads will vary a bit. But no matter the variation, you have no doubt about which family of sharks they belong to because of their uniqueness. Simply put, hammerheads are different. They're special.

Just like these beautiful creatures, the successful also have a way about them that goes far beyond their looks, their possessions, and their friends. They too are different and have distinctive characteristics that set them apart. Just like the hammerhead, there is a uniqueness about those dedicated to living a successful life, and high achievers are not like the average person. When you begin to pursue and attain success, you'll also receive criticism from others and may be labeled as ambitious, lucky, or maybe even a little weird. I wouldn't have it any other way!

Luckily, unlike the hammerhead shark, it's not necessary that you be born this way because success characteristics are available for anyone to acquire. It is something that can be learned and developed.

Next Steps

The next section of this book covers the six elements in great detail. Each of these chapters focuses on just one of the elements at a time and will offer insights into their importance to success and how to apply them. You'll find both philosophical explanations as well as practical and simple ways to get started. The chapters will go in the order found in the phrase SHARK Belief with one exception. I take the "A" first and begin by going over Aim since that is the starting point of the SHARK Belief Success Code. You first need a target or a goal upon which you will focus the other five elements. However, there really is no right or wrong order and you will learn that these all work in harmony and are all simultaneously active. They synergize with one another and each element is made more powerful when applied alongside all of the others.

After reviewing the six elements I'll provide a quick guide on how to get started in applying SHARK Belief to your life. One thing to keep in mind while learning this is that it is essentially about personal development. It's about making personal progress and by definition that means it's about change. I could teach you everything you've ever wanted to know about success, but unless you are willing to take action and implement these ideas, you will never make any progress. It requires more than just theorizing and dreaming big. The thing about success is that beyond the core elements and ideas is the required action and energy to make it happen. You have to execute!

SHARK Belief is about designing the life you want by using the simple framework I lay out. However, don't confuse simple with easy. I never claim that success is easy and the reality is that it's not. It will take work and persistence. You will likely have temporary setbacks but you must persevere. You may not be able to dictate how every event of your life will turn out from here but you CAN change your trajectory and begin moving in ANY direction that you choose. This doesn't mean you have to do a complete 180 degree change but rather, it's about make the small adjustments over time. Just like a plane flying across the country, a slight shift to its flight path will take the plane to a much different destination. The trajectory change may not be noticeable at first, but after several hundred miles, it's a huge difference. You have so much more control over your life than you realize. I'm betting that deep down, you already know that, otherwise you wouldn't be reading this book. You're reading this because there is something more you want to achieve. You're reading this because you know there is great potential in your life and you wish to make the most of it. Perhaps what you've done in the past didn't work exactly as you had hoped, but you're not ready to give up on your dreams and goals. If you're still with me, then I'm confident you're open to change and I know that the SHARK Belief Success Code will work for you!

CHAPTER THREE

Aim High and Focus

"The one trait that all successful people possess is the ability to set and accomplish goals."

- John Dumas

On July 30, 1947, a boy was born in the post-WWII Austrian village of Thal. He had a typical Austrian childhood of those days and one of the highlights of his youth was when the family bought a refrigerator. He was the son of a poor but strict and devout Roman Catholic family and his father pushed him to play several sports as a boy. At age ten, he began dreaming of moving to the United States to achieve success, fame and fortune. At age 14, he decided to choose bodybuilding as his career, resulting in great disappointment and criticism from his parents.

After three years of intense training, he officially started his competitive bodybuilding career at 17 and would subsequently go on to win the Mr. Universe title a few years later. Winning this title would make him the youngest ever Mr. Universe at the age of 20 and it would be a title he would go on to win three more times. Although he spoke very little English, by age 21, bodybuilding would help him realize his dream of moving to the United States and he would eventually become one of the most famous and successful men of his time.

Arnold Schwarzenegger would go on to win the Mr. Olympia contest seven times becoming one of bodybuilding's icons and would help propel the sport into mainstream popularity. His life story is an inspirational example of success and the power of goals to help reach your dreams. Arnold Schwarzenegger was a big believer in the power of goal setting and has achieved some huge goals throughout this life. Schwarzenegger always aimed high and wanted to be the best at whatever field he was pursuing. He is most famous for his bodybuilding accomplishments, acting career and for becoming the Governor of California. What is not as well known about Arnold Schwarzenegger is that he was a prolific goal setter and would always set big goals, which also helped him to succeed as a businessman and investor, as a movie producer and director, as a writer and now as a philanthropist.

When focusing on bodybuilding, his goal was to be the greatest bodybuilder in the world, and this meant winning the Mr. Olympia contest. At age 23, he became the youngest person to ever win the competition and would go on to win the title a total of seven times before finally retiring from bodybuilding. When moving from bodybuilding into acting, he again aimed for the top by setting a goal for a lead acting role despite his thick accent, long name and unusual body. He got his breakthrough when he starred in the box-office hit Conan the Barbarian. Then, just two years later, he would take what some consider his acting career's signature role, and star as the Terminator, making him one of the highest-paid movie actors of all time.

After several decades of acting in and producing films, Schwarzenegger would once again shift his aim by going into politics. Instead of working his way up the legislative ladder, he once again set a big goal by going straight for the Governorship of California in 2003. This would make him one of the most powerful politicians in the country and he would go on to win re-election in 2006 despite his political party being out of favor that year. One of the keys to Arnold Schwarzenegger's success was his Aim. He set big goals, he was never afraid to fail and he dedicated his energy and focus on accomplishing them.

Aim – Why Success Requires Focus

How does aim fit into SHARK Belief? The A in SHARK represents the word Aim. The aim is simply your goal or the desired state of achievement that you're pursuing. Coaches, teachers and authors will use a variety of words to describe this element. They might call it your life's purpose, your long-term goal or your primary desire. Napoleon Hill spoke of goals and aim in life in his books *The Law of Success* and *Think and Grow Rich*. He wrote:

"Any definite chief aim that is deliberately fixed in the mind and held there, with the determination to realize it, finally saturates the subconscious mind until it automatically influences the physical action of the body toward the attainment of that purpose."

He is describing the power of our thoughts and subconscious mind which I'll discuss in depth later but notice that it all begins with first defining an aim. The first step to achieving success is to determine exactly what you want to accomplish. The power behind your aim is in its definition. It's about being definite with what you want and having an exact date for its attainment. As you work the SHARK Belief process, you will also have a definite plan for successfully reaching your aim. If SHARK Belief were represented by a pyramid, then your Aim would be the pinnacle toward which all of the other elements work in harmony to achieve.

Why Goals are Critical to Success

Goals are incredibly important to success and the reason can be summarized in one word, focus. Without a definite chief aim and focus in life, you will spread yourself out too thin by chasing many things at once, which will then divide your attention and focus. You'll either fail to reach any of your goals or you will at best have mediocre results. I've made this mistake in the past by thinking I could set several big goals at once and would try to juggle many priorities at once. I would always underestimate how much time and energy just one of those objectives would require and as a result, I would often feel the stress of trying to keep up and would ultimately experience burnout. Then, I would give up on the goals or I would settle for subpar performance. This was no way to achieve the levels of success I wanted and I soon discovered that I could reach my goals sooner and with better results if I pursued just one major goal at a time. My fear was always in missing an opportunity or wasting time by working on just one goal at a time. But what I found was that by trying to do it all at once, I ended up achieving very little and often felt deep frustration and discouragement.

We have to be realistic and understand that until we internalize the SHARK Belief way of life and prove that we can increase our productivity levels, we first have to go a little bit slower than we want and focus on just one or two things. When pursuing your goals, you will discover that you also have to make time for work, exercise, chores and enjoying quality time with friends and family. Even the most disciplined person can only do so many things at once time before their performance starts to suffer. In fact, you'll find that the most disciplined individuals actually restrict outside distractions and only focus on just one or two major goals at a time.

I love learning new things, I get excited about the opportunities I see everywhere and I'm prone to jump into new things right away. Once I realized this trait about myself, I discovered that regularly reminding myself of my goal and staying focused on the big picture gave me greater satisfaction and also helped me to get much more done in the same amount of time. I mention in the Habits chapter that self-discipline and willpower are one of the greatest determining factors of success and that's because they drive focus and deliberate action. The good news is that willpower is also like a muscle or skill and it can be improved over time. However, until you get to that point, do yourself a favor and limit distractions by staying focused on pursuing a single goal. It's ironic, but sometimes you have to say no to be able to say yes to more things later.

Having a defined aim will give you the focus to pursue only those activities that are critical to achieving your primary goal. The late Steve Jobs put it beautifully when he said, "People think focus means saying yes to the thing you've got to focus on. But that's not what it means at all. It means saying no to the hundred other good ideas that there are. You have to pick carefully. I'm actually as proud of the things we haven't done as the thing I have done. Innovation is saying no to 1,000 things."

It is the same with our goals. You must have a single big pursuit that will drive all other efforts. If you have too many objectives and priorities, then you really don't have any at all.

In his book *What They Don't Teach You in the Harvard Business School*, Mark McCormack wrote about a study on goal setting that was conducted at Harvard University. What they discovered about the truth of goal setting and its impact on performance is incredibly insightful.

"Only 3 percent of the graduates had written goals and plans; 13 percent had goals, but they were not in writing; and a whopping 84 percent had no specific goals at all. Ten years later, the members of the class were interviewed again, and the findings, while somewhat predictable, were nonetheless astonishing. The 13 percent of the class who had goals were earning, on average, twice as much as the 84 percent who had no goals at all. And what about the three percent who had clear, *written* goals? They were earning, on average, TEN TIMES as much as the other 97 percent put together." (Emphasis mine)

Incredible! There is no debating that goals are critical to success and this is why Aim is the starting point of SHARK Belief. You must first set a goal if you wish to achieve success. The sad truth is that 95% of the general population does not have written goals. Most people just go through life reacting to events and getting from one crisis to the next. If you want to be part of the 5% and achieve the levels of success that most only dream of, then you will have to do what 95% of others will not do. You start by setting clear written goals.

Goals Overcome Distractions and Discouragement

"What you think about the longest, becomes the strongest."

- Les Brown

Without a definite goal to keep you focused, you will also become susceptible to outside influences that will change your direction or interests from one day to the next. There is always the latest hot business trend. The grass sometimes does seem greener on the other side and everyone is fighting for your attention. Knowing exactly what you are pursuing and what success looks like for you will help you to persevere when the temptation to quit is strong.

One of the reasons most people fail to reach their goals is because their objectives are not specific enough to let them know when they've reached them. With a vague goal, it's too easy to modify it or just throw it out for another pursuit. Now let me clarify that I also believe your goals will change over time as you grow and that you should be a little flexible and adjust as needed. However, if your goal is too vague and too flexible, then I would argue that it's not really a goal at all. Without a concrete definition of what your goal it, you will be more likely to quit at the first sign of difficulty and will never press through the tough times required to achieve success in any field.

You have to know what you want and why you want it. Your reasons may change over time, but you need to start somewhere. In fact, your plan or method for reaching your goal will likely change as you learn more, but your ultimate goal should remain steady.

My difficulty had always been on deciding what I wanted and having to choose just one path. By using SHARK Belief, I can now organize myself more effectively, which in turn will allow me to achieve more in the same amount of time. That wasn't always the case for me and I first had to prove it to myself by pursuing and accomplishing just ONE goal. It's now much easier for me to do more at once. As your knowledge of SHARK Belief improves, you too can strive for multiple goals at once, but for now, it is in your best interest to first prove to yourself that this system works and that is best done by focusing on achieving just one goal. Make it a simple goal if you must, but put SHARK Belief to the test and it will give you greater confidence when aiming for bigger goals later.

Have a SMART Goal

A good goal will give you clarity. When you have a well-defined objective, it will be easy to know when you have been successful. Answer the following question: "How will I know when I've reached my goal?" The answer to that question will help you describe your goal better and help you refine your written goal statement. The simpler and easier the goal is to remember, the better. Once you've defined your goal statement, rephrase it so that is in the present tense and written as if you've already achieved it. Doing so will help you modify your Beliefs and will also put your subconscious mind to work on formulating a plan to achieve your goal. More on that later.

There are a few variants but I like the following version of the S.M.A.R.T methodology for defining your goal. Your goal should be:

S – Specific

M – Measurable

A – Attainable

R – Relevant

T – Time-bound

Specific so that it's clear what you want and so you'll know when you've achieved it. Measurable means that you can track progress along the way. Attainable means being realistic about timing or probability. I'm all for thinking big, but be realistic about what you can achieve at this point in your life. Attainable is different for everyone and this will change with your level of experience and knowledge. Relevant means your goal should be compatible with your greater vision, your values and your reasons for wanting to reach this aim. If you don't have passion behind it or if your achieving this goal does not move you in the direction you wish to go, then why pursue it? Time-bound is simply putting a deadline or target for when you want to reach your goal. Don't be afraid of a little pressure, as that will help you.

The Most Important Step in Defining Your Aim

The final step in establishing a good goal statement is to *physically* write it down. This is NOT negotiable! Writing out your goal statement is the most important part of setting a goal and if you fail to do this, it will be as if you never set a goal in the first place. I won't bore you with the scientific explanation, but there but there is a deep mind-body connection that occurs when you physically write down your goal and subsequently read it out loud. This has been researched extensively and was even written about in the 1920's by the likes of Napoleon Hill and Wallace D. Wattles. It is the first step in turning your thoughts into reality. Bring your dreams to life by first writing out your definite aim in the form of a detailed goal statement.

Out of Sight, Out of Mind

We've all heard the saying "out of sight, out of mind." Usually, it's about something you're supposed to do but simply forget about because you're not thinking about it. It's like that chore that keeps getting put off or the person you keep forgetting to call. Without a reminder or something to keep you focused on what you need to do, it'll simply stay out of mind and probably never get done. Take the typical New Year's resolution that is so commonly set every January. Perhaps you'll say something like, "My New Year's Resolution is to eat more salads this year." But then you never write it down, or even if you do, you'll never look at it again.

What happens next is that you won't think about your new resolution very often and it will be out of mind. Within a few weeks, you will have all but given up on doing this. It has now gone out of sight and is very out of mind. The reality is that this is what happens to most goals. They are not reviewed often enough and despite the best intentions and time spent planning out the goal in detail, they will be forgotten and overcome by the busyness of life.

To win, you must reverse this and keep your goal in mind at all times. At a minimum, you should review and read your primary objective once a day. Always remind yourself where you're going and what your bigger vision is. It may only take you a few seconds or even a couple of minutes, but the power of reading your goal every day is incredibly helpful to programming the subconscious mind and for directing your daily actions. Sales coach Grant Cardone tells of how he physically writes down his goals twice a day, both in the morning and before going to bed, and he also writes them again when he has a failure or setback. You can bet he knows where he is going and what his priorities are! Grant Cardone has achieved incredible success on several levels and takes his goal reviewing seriously.

Even if you don't start your goal reviewing routine at Grant Cardone's level right away, you should still make time to read your goals frequently and keep yourself focused on the bigger picture. This is especially important during times of failure or discouragement. It will keep you moving forward. If you really want success, you should never let your goal be out of sight or out of mind.

Remember, there are six core elements to success with SHARK Belief and Aim is just one. The others will work in harmony together to move you toward your chosen aim so it's important to always be mindful of what you want to achieve. It ultimately becomes your why for the other five areas and acts as a magnetic force that keeps you focused and pulls you in the direction of your choosing. The successful did not achieve their major accomplishments in life by accident. They knew what they wanted and began taking action to move in that direction. It also required hard work and persistence but their achievement was certainly deliberate. It all starts with a goal in mind.

The Target Seeking Mind

The heat-seeking missile was first introduced in WWII and was a big advancement from the traditional point and shoot weapons or dropping clusters of bombs. Over the decades, this technology continued to develop and soon created a small and compact version. One of the most famous is the shoulder-fired Stinger missile and was used extensively against enemy aircraft during the 1980's Soviet war in Afghanistan. The CIA supplied large quantities of this weapon to the Afghan rebels, and it has been said that the Stinger was responsible for over half of the Soviet aircraft losses during that war.

The way it works is the missile is given a target aircraft that it then "locks onto". Once it is fired, it will track the infrared heat signatures of its target and adjust its trajectory as it moves closer and closer. The missile may appear to be moving in a smooth fashion but what is actually happening in split seconds, are thousands of sensor readings sending instructions back to the missile's controls, which then make adjustments to its flight path. There is a "seeker" element at the front of the missile, which is critical to keeping it moving in the right direction and giving it such a high success rate. Even a fast-moving target such as a jet or helicopter will find it difficult to escape the high-speed tracking of this target-seeking missile. The Stinger is designed as a goal-seeking mechanism with the ultimate aim of reaching the enemy target and detonating its warhead.

Much like this Stinger missile, a human mind is an incredible machine that will also function as a goal-seeking mechanism when it's been given an aim to pursue. It is literally wired for attaining success. The problem is that we usually fail to use our mind for this purpose and we allow outside influences to redirect our focus and lead us down a random path. Remember that when you first set a goal, you do not need to know exactly how you will attain it or which way you will ultimately take. Do let that stop you and certainly don't let it determine how big of a goal you want to achieve either.

What is important is that you first know what your goal is. Once you determine your goal and begin to review it regularly, your subconscious mind will start to go to work to identify opportunities or information that will help you begin moving in the right direction. You will start to notice things you didn't before. You'll meet just the right person to help you get started. You'll come across a book or video with the exact information you needed. You'll suddenly be "attracting" things into your life that will help you reach your goal.

You've experienced this phenomenon when buying a new car. A few months before the purchase, you didn't really notice that model on the road as much. However, the day after you buy your new car, you suddenly notice the exact car everywhere you go! What changed? Was there a sudden increase in the number of people wanting the exact type of car you now drive? Of course not, they were always out there but your mind was just not trained to notice them. It's the same with your goals. Once you begin to focus on what you want, you'll start to see things that will help you and you'll also attract those things into your life. That is why I said to not worry about having a plan for how you will achieve your goal when you first set it. As long as you stay focused on it, you will begin to get the info you need for that plan. The other elements of SHARK Belief are designed to help you do just that.

Quick Take-Aways

You must have an Aim - Aim in SHARK Belief represents your goal, your purpose or mission. All success begins by first defining what it is you want to achieve and then focusing your energy on pursuing that goal. Be specific about what you want to achieve and make it a S.M.A.R.T goal.

Start with Just One Major Goal – Most successful people focus on just one primary goal at a time. Remember, Aim is about providing clarity and focus. By pursuing several goals at once, you dissipate your energy over many things and end up achieving none of them. At best, you'll have mediocre results.

Think Big, Start Small – Don't worry about how you will achieve your goal at the time you set it. Be willing to fail but think big and pursue big goals if you want massive success. However, if this is your first time really aiming for a goal or if you're new to SHARK Belief, then start with a small or simple goal so that you really get the process down.

Make it Real – Remember the first step in transforming your dreams into reality is to start the creation process by physically writing down your goal. Then you must review it regularly and read it out loud. Memorize your goal and say it to yourself often. It's all about making the goal real in your mind first, and then making it real in your life.

CHAPTER FOUR

How to Succeed with Skills

"The separation of talent and skill is one of the greatest misunderstood concepts for people who are trying to excel, who have dreams, who want to do things. Talent you have naturally. Skill is only developed by hours and hours and hours of beating on your craft."

- Will Smith

Among the world's most highly trained and skilled people are the members of the Special Forces groups and elite military units from around the world. Almost every branch of the military has at least one Special Forces group. One of the most popular and well-known groups are the United States Navy SEALs. In his book *Lone Survivor*, Marcus Luttrell gives his eyewitness account of a 2005 reconnaissance mission in Afghanistan that resulted in the largest loss of life in Navy SEAL history. The mission quickly went awry when the team was discovered by a group of herders who later revealed their position to Taliban fighters. The Taliban then attacked the SEALs with machine guns, rocket-propelled grenades, and mortars. It's an incredible story culminating in a harrowing firefight that demonstrates courage and sacrifice of the SEALs, valiantly fighting side by side until Luttrell was the only one left alive.

Earlier in the account, Lutrell goes into fascinating detail about the rigors of Navy SEAL qualification and the intensive specialized training they receive, which has become legendary for the extreme physical and mental challenges one must endure. Only 25% of the trainees make it through the training. It is widely considered to be the most physically and mentally demanding military training in existence. Over the course of 30 months, candidates undergo a brutally intense training regimen that prepares them to handle just about any mission they are called to perform, including parachuting, SCUBA diving, combat swimming, reconnaissance, navigation, mountaineering, demolitions, tactical & sniper assaults, hostage rescue, hand to hand combat, and even performing medical treatment.

The number of skills a Navy SEAL will learn during training is almost incomprehensible and will include significant mental skills such as the use of high-tech devices, intelligence gathering and analysis, survival skills, and learning new languages. The SEALs are forced to learn these skills under intense pressure and stress and while also pushing their body's physical limits.

In Lone Survivor, Luttrell tells of his survival following the deaths of his comrades. By the time an RPG literally launched him down a mountainside and into hiding, he had already sustained multiple bone fractures, gunshot wounds, and a broken back. Still, he managed to crawl down a ravine, cross a river, and hide for several hours before finally being sheltered by friendly villagers. Luttrell attributed his survival to his extensive training and skills. It was not that his body was superhuman or vastly superior to the average person's; rather, it was his mind that had been transformed by the intensive training and the incredible skill acquisition he had undergone. He recalls that one of his training instructors shouted, "The body can take damn near anything. It's the mind that needs training!"

Luttrell was able to stay alive because when he was at his weakest point and all hope seemed lost, his training and skills took over and did what they were intended to do; keep him alive. It's no wonder why these warriors represent one of the most feared combat forces in the world.

How to Succeed with Skills

The S in SHARK Belief is for Skills. Success in any field will require that you develop particular skills that are specific to your aim. Often, success requires a combination of several essential skills. One thing you will find in common amongst all of the ultra-successful is that they are all highly skilled. For example, entrepreneur and author Grant Cardone is a world-class salesman, and Steve Jobs had incredible presentation and communication skills. The world's top CEOs are all skilled leaders. Many successful tech entrepreneurs started because of their technical or programming skills, while others have had a keen ability to organize the activity and efforts of others.

The more skillful you become, the more effective you will be at reaching your desired results. For any entrepreneur looking to build the next world-changing start-up, skills such as pitching and selling, communication, leadership, technical skills, and the ability to focus are all essentials in those early days and necessary for building a successful company. Even non-business goals such as learning a new language, learning to play the guitar, or finishing your first marathon will require that you understand and develop the techniques necessary to accomplish them.

When it comes to learning new skills, SHARK Belief takes a reverse-engineering approach to help you determine the specific skills you'll need. Instead of finding out what you're good at now and picking some skills to compliment your strengths, first determine exactly what your desired outcome is and then determine the skills you will need. Once you know what you're trying to accomplish, you can begin planning how to achieve your goal, and that may reveal that you need to acquire new skills.

Remember, the order should be to first to decide the "what," and then determine the "how." As the old saying goes, start with the end in mind. Most people take the opposite approach and say, "I've always been good at drawing and painting so maybe I'll use this skill and build a business around it." Even worse, others will say things like, "I've never been a good sales person or a good leader" so they avoid setting any goals or starting businesses that will require those skills. Please, don't limit your life by only doing what you've always been good at or what you're comfortable with. You are way more capable than you can ever imagine! Never be afraid to learn new skills. We all can learn new things and this chapter will give you some tips for accelerated learning.

Regardless of the goal you've set for yourself, you will need to identify and cultivate the skills that are specific to reaching your goal. If your current skills don't align with your purpose, then they are of limited use. For example, if you aim to be a world-class public speaker and success coach, then being extremely skilled in software engineering doesn't do you much good! Your skills are part of the toolset you will leverage to reach your goals.

All industries, professions, and even hobbies will have one or two essential skills that, if mastered, will put you at an elite level and all but ensure success. It is often the lack of skill that holds people back. Many people overestimate just how good they really are and may not be good enough to reach the levels of success desired. Could it be that learning just one skill is what has been holding you back? Reflect upon some failed attempts and examine whether it was a missing skill that caused you to come up short. Perhaps you were working extremely hard, you networked with the right people, read the right books and even worked on your beliefs through visualization and affirmations, yet you still did not succeed. Why? Maybe you thought you had developed the level of skill necessary, but in fact you had a lot more learning to do?

Examine all of the six elements of SHARK Belief and be sure you've factored all of them in. In my own experience, it was a shortage in skills that contributed to my early failures. The first couple of businesses I started could have benefited greatly from a strong web-presence and digital marketing but I was unfamiliar with how to market online or even how to update a simple webpage. Unfortunately, I was also too cheap to hire someone with these skills and I was "too busy" to bother learning how to do it myself. Once I recognized this shortage in skills and knowledge, I began to correct them and the results also began to change for the better. The price however was a loss of time and potential business growth. Don't make my mistake. Take a hard look at the skills that will set you apart and consider spending some serious time learning them. At the very least, make sure you bridge any gap in skills by partnering with someone that has those you need.

Anyone can become skilled!

I know what you're thinking. "I wasn't born with skills," or "I don't have any natural talents. I've never been good at this or that." Stop! If you remember nothing else about this chapter, remember this one thing: Being born with "talent" is a myth.

All highly skilled individuals got there through deliberate practice and hard work. Additionally, anyone can learn new skills and become great, including you! I understand that some people were born with genetic advantages that lend themselves to particular skills, or that having a knack for certain things makes it easier to learn them. However, being skilled is always superior to being talented and this so-called "natural talent" can be outworked and beaten by highly developed skills.

There's an old saying that says "even the master was once a beginner". Unfortunately, most people tend to have a flawed belief that if they're not already good at something, then they will never be good at it. It sounds silly, but think about it. Have you ever said, "Oh, I've never been good at sales," or "I've never been a good public speaker"? Well, then ask yourself if you've ever taken training in these areas. Have you committed to developing those skills, or even gone as far as working with a coach or mentor? If the answer is no, then of course you've never been good at those things! Anyone good at those things is always working at them and has likely been working hard for years.

The right mindset is critical to success. It's especially crucial in learning new skills. Believing that you can never be good at something just because you're not good at it right now is a limiting belief and a huge reason many people never reach their full potential. Remember that you didn't always know how to walk, ride a bike, or swim. Learning new skills shouldn't stop after childhood. A common theme you'll see in SHARK Belief is that it doesn't matter who or where you are right now because SHARK Belief is about change, growth, and ongoing personal development. If you have a dream and now realize that it requires you to develop new skills, you should be happy to know that those skills are in reach if you want them bad enough. You don't have to be born talented, and there are many strategies that can help you start developing new skills very quickly. I'll go into more detail about the myth of inborn talent, and will also share some of the essential techniques to help you develop skills quickly. Just remember, if others have done it, then you can too.

"You don't have to be great to get started, but you have to get started to be great."

- Les Brown

More than Passion

Successfully reaching your aim requires a lot more than a deep desire for it. Many people believe that if they just want something bad enough, that if they think about it day and night, talk about frequently, and work hard, that they too will ultimately achieve their goal. The problem is that unless you identify and develop the skills required for attaining success in your chosen field, then failure will probably be the result. The truth is that a lot of people want it. A lot of people REALLY want it and are also passionately working hard at success, but passion and desire alone will not get results. It takes more than passion. It takes skills! People often blame poor results on bad relationships, a bad economy, or just plain bad luck. They rarely stop to do some serious self-analysis to see if failure was due to lack of skill.

To reach success, your actions must be focused and deliberate. Every goal, every field of work, and every pursuit will require a certain level of skillfulness. There are different levels of skillfulness and not all skills will require you to reach the master level. Some are merely simple techniques that will help you along the way. However, those that reach the highest level of success in their fields are often the most skilled, and experts in one or two areas. Yes, they have passion for their work and a deep desire to reach their goals, but they also understand that passion alone won't do it. As Arnold Schwarzenegger says, success also requires hard, hard work!

Skills are a byproduct of knowledge, with habits set in place to help develop them. I want to emphasize this critical point so I'll state it again: A central theme in SHARK Belief is that success requires change. Sometimes it's little more than a small adjustment; changing just one thing. Other times, it's drastic and disruptive. However, even big changes in our lives are usually done by small and seemingly insignificant modifications over a period of time. Stagnation is the most dangerous place to be, and you must always be in the mode where you're growing and improving yourself.

If you think you've learned all you will ever need to know or that you've developed all of the skills you'll ever need, then I'm afraid you're in for a huge surprise. Technology will continue to disrupt, and that change will be an enormous opportunity for some and a crisis for others. Because you're reading this, I highly doubt that you're done growing.

I also realize that many of you will read this and doubt your ability to gain new skills and master those necessary for success. I know there are some of you who believe you don't have any natural talents or that it would be impossible for you to master a skill that you really suck at right now. Read on! I will disprove some of those theories and also give you some practical tips on how to acquire the skills you need to reach your goals.

Talent vs Skill

"If people knew how hard I had to work to gain my mastery, it would not seem so wonderful at all."

- Michelangelo

The idea that certain individuals possess a God-given talent or natural-born ability is almost universally accepted. We believe that talent is something people are born with and that if you don't already have it, then you can't acquire it. When watching the Olympics, we marvel at all of the talented people vying for the top spot in the world, or when enjoying a musical performance, we are awestruck by how gifted some people are. In college we're pressed to find out what our "talents" are and build a career around our passions. We'll quickly rule out several fields because we've concluded that we lack certain aptitudes or that we've never been good at a particular thing such as number calculations or artistic creativity. Sadly, these conclusions are often based on our own limiting experiences of having given a half-hearted effort for a few weeks only to quit soon after that.

Could it be that natural talent is not really that common? Clearly, certain physical attributes can help some individuals excel in areas where others cannot. If your fully developed body is 4'9 and 130 pounds, then it's unlikely you'll ever play basketball in the NBA, regardless of how good your three-point shooting is. Likewise, if you have the body of an NFL linebacker, then it's going to be pretty hard to excel in gymnastics. However, what we're learning is that even with these small and limited examples of physical advantage, so-called natural talent is not that common, nor is it a predictor of success.

In recent history, a tremendous amount of research has been done on the study of talent to discover why some people have it and others don't. Scientists have even begun to look at our DNA to see if there is a "talent gene" responsible for greatness. The biggest surprise from all of this research has been that more and more evidence is beginning to show that being born with innate abilities is simply a myth. Those we often label as "gifted" or having been born with a natural talent is not due to genetics but rather, they have acquired those skills through circumstance and by hours of deliberate practice. This includes those with seeming high intellect and fantastic memories. These are developed skills that were acquired through training and were not the result of winning the gene-pool lottery.

In his book *Talent is Overrated*, Geoff Colvin examines two famous prodigies, Mozart and Tiger Woods. He illustrates how even these two seemingly gifted individuals were the product of thousands of hours of practice, expert teachers, and the right circumstances. In other words, they weren't born that way. For example, by the time Mozart had written his Piano Concerto No 9 at age 21, he already had been through 18 years of rigorous, expert training. His entire life had been dedicated to music, and his success was the culmination of incredibly hard work over an extended period of time.

One has to ask; would Mozart have become Mozart had he not been the son of the domineering Leopold Mozart, a famous composer, performer, and expert of his era in teaching music to children? Perhaps to the disappointment of Mozart fans, we now know that he was not born with a divine spark of musical genius, but rather it was developed through years of intense training and expert guidance. This in no way takes anything away from the beauty of the music he composed or the greatness he achieved. I personally love listening to works by Mozart. All I'm trying to point out is that we are generally inclined to believe that others are born with great gifts that we can never possess, instead of facing this reality: greatness is not born. It is made.

Another example is the story of Tiger Woods. He was the son of a golf fanatic whose skills ranked among the top 10% in the world. Tiger's father loved to teach and was eager to begin showing his son the game of golf as soon as he could. When Tiger was only a few months old, he would sit in his high chair and watch his father hit golf balls into a net for hours on end. Before Tiger turned two, he and his father were already practicing and playing golf regularly. By age four, little Tiger was already receiving professional coaching. Before turning twenty, Tiger Woods had already amassed seventeen years of intense and consistent practice. By this point, he had put in more practice hours than most golfers will in their entire lives! It's no wonder he was able to achieve such international recognition and achievement at such a young age. The same argument could be made for other greats such as Michelangelo, Serena Williams and Bobby Fisher.

If we believe that natural talent is required for success and that it's been given to only a few luckily recipients, then we'll use that as an excuse and we'll never reach the levels of success we dream of. However, if we accept what research proves, and embrace the belief that greatness and success are by-products of things that are largely in our control, then we can begin to build the skills necessary for reaching our goals.

As it turns out, skills and knowledge are not the result of natural gifts or being born smart. Rather, they are the result of consistent and deliberate practice. Furthermore, it is skills and not talent that matters most when working towards a goal.

The good news is that anyone can acquire new skills and even reach the elite level if done correctly. The bad news for some is that there is no easy street and it will almost always require extended periods of practice and hard work. Luckily, reaching the master-level in all skills isn't necessary. Rather, focus on the one or two specific skills that will help you the most in reaching your goal. The more skilled you are in these chosen areas, the better.

To truly become great at one or two skills, you will need dedicated and concentrated effort. If you try to gain skills in too many things, your efforts will be scattered and you will only achieve mediocre results. As with most of the elements in SHARK Belief, focus is the key to effective implementation. So let go of the notion that you have to be talented before you can become skilled, and instead, identify that skill which will help you the most and get working on developing it. The sooner you do this, the sooner you will reach your goals.

Time Requirement for Learning a New Skill

So how long does it take to learn a new skill? We're all busy, so the thought of taking the time to acquire a new skill can be intimidating. If you're like me, you would like to learn new things but you also want to know the fastest and most efficient way to learn. In Malcolm Gladwell's 2008 book *Outliers*, he discusses a famous study done by the Swedish psychologist Anders Ericsson, in which he determined the amount of time it takes to master any skill. This is now popularly known as the 10,000-hour rule. Wait, 10,000 hours?! That is a lot of time! To put it into context, a full-time employee will work about 2,000 hours a year. Even a part-time effort of four hours a day for five days a week will translate into 1,000 hours of practice per year. At that pace, it will take you ten years to reach the 10,000-hour mark! Who has ten years for a new skill?!

Before you freak out and give up on your goal, let's take a closer look at what the research really says. It turns out it takes nowhere near 10,000 hours to learn a new skill. Dr. Ericsson was studying the experts in their respective fields to determine how long it took to master that skill. He studied professional athletes, world-class musicians, chess grandmasters and the like. In other words, Ericsson found that it takes 10,000 hours of deliberate practice to get to the top in an ultra-competitive field and on a very narrow subject. He did not conclude that it takes 10,000 hours to become good or even very good at a particular skill. Rather, he was referring to those at the pinnacle of their fields - the very best in the world. He was talking about what it took to become a Mozart or Roger Federer.

Most of us don't learn a new skill with the intent of becoming the top 1% in the world, so unless you plan on competing against Tiger Woods in the PGA, there's no reason you would need to master the game at that level.

So do you really need to reach 10,000 hours before you can start working on your goals? Absolutely not! All you need is to identify the one or two most valuable skills in your field, and get to work. If you are building your first start-up, you will need technical skills specific to your industry. Perhaps you'll need to refine your public speaking ability or your sales skills. Perhaps you need more marketing ability. This type of goal-specific analysis will be different for everyone, but once you know what your goal is, the specific skills you need quickly become evident. For most entrepreneurs, it usually comes down to one or two essential skills that will make the difference between success and failure. Those are the ones you want to begin developing first.

The Different Levels of Skill Competence

So then, how long does it take to learn a new skill? Well, we know it doesn't take 10,000 hours. The other extreme says that new skills can be learned in as little as 20 hours of deep and deliberate practice. The short answer is that it depends on the skill's complexity but generally speaking, you'd be surprised at how quickly most people can acquire a new skill. Tim Ferriss, the author of *The 4-Hour Work Week*, is famous for experimenting with hacks to quickly learn new skills. He even made a complete show about it called the Tim Ferriss Experiment where he pushes the limits of human potential by learning a new skill each week. Similarly, author and speaker Josh Kaufman shares some strategies for rapid skill acquisition in his book *The First 20 Hours*.

We'll look at both of their strategies in detail but the point of rapid skill acquisition is not to become an expert in as little as 20 hours but rather, to break down a skill into its essential elements and learn those that will give you the most return for your time invested. Some of the techniques go against conventional teaching but many are just common sense and are excellent ways to get started quickly. Remember, it's about skill acquisition, not skill mastery.

There are different levels of competence for any skill so it's common sense that some people are more skilled at a particular thing than others. You will be somewhere in between "I know absolutely nothing about that" and "I'm the best in the world at that." Just how good you need to be will depend on what you want to accomplish. You may need to become extremely skilled at one thing while only needing to be 'good enough' at another in order to reach your goals.

Note that this is not a pass to be the jack-of-all-trades and master of none. While you may develop a long list of skills, in order to be successful you must leverage the one or two skills in which you develop an exceptional proficiency. The more skilled you are at something that others value, and the more you leverage that skill to accomplish your goals, the higher degree of success you will have.

When you first start off at acquiring a new skill, you may find yourself at the very low end of the learning curve (i.e. you really suck at this!) Or you may already be somewhere along the mediocre to pretty good line. The learning curve merely illustrates the time it takes to move up in skill level. With some skills, you'll go up to high proficiency in a shorter time, but with other skills, it may take much longer. You'll notice that one quickly goes from being really bad at something to being pretty good. Then progress slows down, and it takes a little longer to go from good to really good. At that point the learning curve really begins to plateau, and it takes a lot longer to go from very good to expert level. This is where the 10,000-hour rule comes in. The first 20 hours is about moving along the path from being really bad to getting pretty good in a relatively short period of time.

Your goal may require that you only get past the basic level. However, most people will give up long before that point because the very nature of learning new skills feels uncomfortable. It's hard at first. No one likes to feel stupid, and learning anything new often makes us feel incompetent and subpar. By pre-committing to at least 20 hours of focused and deliberate training before deciding to give up, you almost guarantee that you'll get past that initial feeling of inadequacy, and will learn the basics. Once you get some of the basics down, you'll find renewed motivation to keep going because you'll begin to see and believe that you can learn that new skill. Bear in mind that it is deliberate practice and concentrated effort that determine how skilled you become. It has nothing to do with genes or natural talent or even spending more time on practice. Having more years of experience isn't necessarily a predictor of greater skill because many people plateau after a while and are just maintaining current levels rather than continuing to getting better. No one is born skilled, and just spending more time on something will not guarantee that you'll continue to get better at it. If you commit to the 20 hours, make sure those 20 hours are spent on skill-building activity that pushes you and not on doing that which you're already good at.

Types of Skills

Not all skills are created equal. You will find some that are easier for you, while others will take a lot more work. You will no doubt need a combination of skills to achieve your aim, and this will include both hard skills and soft skills. Most big skills will actually include a mix of the two. For example, most professional sports have a very clear set of motor skills required for success, but there is also a crucial cognitive set of competencies that will often be the differentiator between the winners and losers. Being able to think quickly and change strategies or make split-second decisions are the types of soft skills that can take years of experience to develop but when used in conjunction with the hard motor skills, can give an athlete the winning advantage.

Hard Skills Vs. Soft Skills

Hard skills include technical skills, such as understanding the basic syntax of a programming language or reading financial statements, as well as motor skills, which require physical movement, coordination, or finesse. Swinging a golf club, playing a musical instrument, or touch-typing area are all motor skills. The best way to develop these is through repetition and through slow concentrated action so that you know when you're making mistakes and to get a deep understanding of it. It's better to move very slowly at first and learn how to get it right rather than doing a high number of sloppy repetitions.

Soft skills are cognitive skills and those requiring mental ability such as creativity, decision-making, pattern recognition, or problem solving. Cognitive skills are knowledge-based skills, generally developed through learning to recognize patterns and potential solutions by testing yourself and by training in varying environments or situations. Memorization helps, but finding new ways to continually challenge yourself will help you develop even quicker. A good example of this would be sales training: knowing how to respond to various concerns and questions a prospective customer would have. This also includes all those soft skills such as leadership, communication and interpersonal or social skills.

You will need both. Just as elite Navy SEALs are required to master both hard and soft skills, the successful entrepreneur will also need a repertoire of both types of skills. Every business professional that has achieved excellence in their industry can claim to have a handful to key skills in each area. I list several to consider mastering toward the end of this chapter.

Keys to Rapid Skill Acquisition

So far we've been talking about how long it takes to learn a new skill because this is usually what everyone considers before deciding whether or not to even start. However, the reality is that it's not about the *quantity* of time but the *quality* of the time invested. The question should not be how long will it take to learn this skill but rather, what is the best way to learn this skill?

Some people may have more experience in an area of expertise, only to see someone new learn the skill and quickly surpass their level of competence. The difference is one person goes through the motions when practicing and is just "putting in time" while the other person is using the same time for deep, concentrated and purposeful practice. Most people would rather practice doing what they can already easily do and just engage in repetition, but if you want to grow, you need to practice doing what you are not good at. That's how you push your skill to the next level. Stay outside of your comfort zone; reach for that target that is just outside of your grasp. You will eventually become good enough to hit that target, and that's when you push the goal out a little further. Don't practicing longer, train smarter. Let's take a look at two of my favorite frameworks for rapid skill acquisition.

The DiSSS approach by Tim Ferriss

Tim Ferriss is one of today's leaders in teaching rapid skill acquisition. He breaks down his framework for accelerated learning into an acronym he calls DiSSS. This stands for Deconstruction, Selection, Sequencing, and Stakes (the "i" just makes it easier to say and remember). Using this model, Ferriss has been able to quickly learn a number of skills including open water swimming, speaking and writing in 6 languages, playing musical instruments, cooking, martial arts, and dancing just to name a few. Here's a quick overview of his process.

Deconstruction

Skill acquisition can become overwhelming and a lot of this is because most skills are actually groupings of many sub-skills. Take the game of golf: various motor skills and techniques go into playing the game such as driving, chipping, and putting which are all entirely different skills. Even having excellent sales skills can be broken down into several key techniques: interpersonal skills, presentation skills, negotiation, and closing skills.

To acquire any new skill quickly, you first need to break down the complex into simple pieces. A little research into a skill will begin to reveal patterns and main ideas that show up repeatedly. If you have trouble identifying them, reach out to others who have the skill you want and learn from them what the fundamental components are. A little research early on in this process will pay huge dividends later as you'll be able to optimize the time you spend practicing by finding shortcuts to the learning process.

Selection

Once you've identified the major components of the skill you want to acquire, the next step is to determine the elements that will have the most impact on your learning and ability. This is sort of like using the Pareto Principle or the 80/20 rule. Take the minimalist approach and begin by using as few tools or techniques as possible. For example, if you're learning to play golf, don't spend practice time learning to chip onto the green or hit out of a sand trap. If a large part of your initial game will be spent hitting with irons along the green, then focus on that first. This will allow you to get started by focusing on just one or two critical areas without feeling overwhelmed or like you need to "know it all." Tim Ferriss explains that this step is about finding the minimum effective dose to effectively acquire a new skill and recommends that one use very few tools and be good with those tools.

Sequencing

This stage is about looking at the order in which you practice the various steps, perhaps changing the conventional approach to learning the skill. For example, professional chess players will train by starting at the end of a game instead of the beginning. Instead of playing a game from the outset and worrying about which opening moves to make, their coaches will set up a board to simulate a partially played game so they can instead focus on other skills such as board control or mating an opponent. In his book, Ferriss explains that when he decided to learn to tango, advice from other male professionals revealed that learning the female role first enhanced their performance as the lead. Learning the follow position first, he says, allowed him to master posture, foot position, and weight shifting before attempting to learn the leading role he had initially botched.

Stakes

Applying stakes to skill acquisition will help with focus and motivation. A big reason people fail to achieve their goals or follow through with learning a new skill is because there aren't any consequences for failing them. Giving yourself real consequences will increase your desire and motivation to learn that new skill. It comes down to accountability. One recommendation Ferriss gives is to use tools such as stickk.com which penalizes you for not completing a goal. On Stickk, a user creates a goal, sets the stakes (typically in the form of money) and chooses an "anti-charity" which will reap the benefits of the money if the objective isn't accomplished. No one likes the thought of giving money to a charity they absolutely disagree with, so they are more inclined to makes sure that doesn't happen by sticking with their goal. Having an accountability partner or another form of external pressure always helps to stay with the learning when it gets tough. There are many apps and websites created to help you do this and I maintain a list of the best ones at SHARKBelief.com.

Another angle to stakes that Tim Ferriss points out is to first practice skills in low-risk situations so that you can focus on just one or two particulars first. For example, if you want to learn how to cook and chop food with a knife like a professional, it's best to practice cutting with a plastic lettuce knife first so you can focus on the chopping technique without having to worry about cutting your fingers. The same goes for business skills. Don't wait to learn the art of sales or negotiations when your living depends on it. Instead, practice in a safe low-risk environment with simulations or role-playing before upping the ante.

Josh Kaufman's First 20 Hours

Josh Kaufman, the author of *The Personal MBA*, also wrote a book on obtaining new skills as quickly and efficiently as possible. The idea is that by approaching learning with some strategy, one can learn just about any skill to a sufficient level with about 20 hours of intensive practice. That's quite the opposite extreme from Gladwell's 10,000 hours, but the key word in Kaufman's approach is learning skills to a sufficient level. He's talking about being competent enough so the skill helps you, but not necessarily to the point where you are considered world-class. Both levels have their place in your toolset but for those skills we need to pick up quickly, this approach works well.

He breaks down his method of learning new skills into the following four steps:

Deconstruct

Just like Tim Ferriss' approach, this step is about breaking down the skill into smaller sub-skills. If you wanted to learn a new language, learning the most common words and phrases will help you to get started. It's already covered above so I won't repeat this step in detail but it's interesting to find that both Ferriss and Kaufman point out the importance of really analyzing the skill you want to learn before getting started.

Learning

Learn just enough about each sub-skill so that you can begin to practice effectively and know enough to self-correct. Once you know how each sub-skill should be successfully performed, you'll know when to spot mistakes and find ways to correct them. It helps to identify or set up fast feedback loops so you know when you're doing something wrong. When learning skills such as programming, this is easy since your program will crash immediately or you'll get an error if done incorrectly. Other skills such as negotiation or presentation skills should be practiced with others so you can get feedback before you attempt a real-world trial.

Remove

Kaufman emphasizes making the learning process as easy as possible by removing any physical, mental, or emotional barriers that get in the way of practice. If you want to learn to play guitar, you'll be more likely to practice every day if you keep the guitar out by your couch or bed rather than having to get it from the top shelf of the backroom closet each night. The same goes with distractions. When I was learning how to code mobile apps, I would turn off my cell phone and email for an hour to minimize the interruptions I would get. A half hour of deep and focused practice will improve your skills faster than practicing for two hours while fighting distractions and interruptions. Remember, it's about the quality of the practice rather than the quantity.

Practice

Commit to practicing the key sub-skills for at least 20 hours. Not just "going through the motions" type of training but 20 hours of deep and concentrated practice. Practicing for just 45 minutes a day will get you past your 20-hour mark within a month. Additionally, this is 20 hours of practice that is stretching you past your comfort zone so you're constantly in learning mode. You'll be amazed at how much you can learn in just the first 20 hours of picking up a new skill.

Kaufman also points out that the best time to practice is right before going to sleep or just before a nap. The reason for this is due to how our brain consolidates new learning while we sleep. You actually perform the skill better after waking up, compared to how you were doing during the prior practice session because your brain has had time to process everything. The same applies to studying and learning new knowledge.

8 Secrets for Rapid Learning & Skill Acquisition

There are a number of ways to quickly learn new skills, and some methods will be more effective than others. However, the following techniques have proven to be the most effective for learning any skill as well as for acquiring new knowledge.

Here are my top picks:

Practice in Shorter Sessions – Studies have shown that it is more effective to learn new skills over a longer period of time using shorter sessions rather than cramming in one long practice session. So instead of practicing or learning for ten hours straight, you'll gain and retain much more by doing twenty 30-minute sessions over a longer period. This is because our brains are better at encoding new information into the synapses in short repeated sessions as opposed to a single large session. This holds true for learning both motor skills and cognitive skills, since all of the learning is ultimately taking place at the neural level of the brain by building and strengthening connections.

Frequent Practice - One key to rapid skill acquisition is to do it as often as possible. You'll gain much more by practicing intensely for just 15 minutes every day instead of practicing for two hours just one day a week. The more time you let pass between practice sessions, the harder it is for your brain to build upon the prior learning. As noted before, your mind learns better with shorter more frequent sessions. If you're pressed for time, don't wait until the weekends to practice; find a little bit of time each day. You want to keep yourself in a constant learning mode, and this is accomplished through consistency. This also helps you remember what you've learned and will keep you motivated since you'll begin to see progress much sooner. The name of the game is to practice whether you feel like it or not. Persistence pays.

Goal Oriented Practice – Instead of trying to practice all of the sub-skills you want to learn during each session, focus on just one area at a time per session and home in on the details of that skill. Additionally, you should have a goal for what you want to accomplish during session. Instead of saying "I will practice for one hour" approach your practice by saying "I will do this entire routine ten times." The key is to set a target of what you want to accomplish and finish it, regardless of how long it takes. Professional athletes take this approach and will often focus on performing a certain number of shots or running through a predetermined number of routines rather than setting a time limit for their practice session.

Keep Notes – Write down notes and thoughts on your progress. By keeping a notebook (paper or virtual) to jot down key ideas and lessons as you learn them, you'll reinforce them in your mind. This will also help you measure your progress. Keeping notes will give you a running history and provide you with a quick view of what is working and what isn't. Journaling and note taking are essential elements to personal growth and are just as important when learning a new skill. At a minimum, I always keep track of the days I've practiced since it provides a nice visual on the time and effort I've devoted to learning. It's very motivating to look back and see a calendar full of multi-day streaks of skill building practice days.

Stay in the Zone – There are three primary mental states or difficulty levels we can be in when learning new skills. The first is our comfort zone and that is basically the maintenance zone. Training in this zone is simply doing what you can already do and is not challenging you much. There's no growth. The comfort zone is typically where most of us like to play because it feels satisfying when we can perform a skill with a high degree of competency. This zone is useful for keeping your current skills fresh but will do little to advance you to the next level.

Next is the learning zone, and this is where you want to be since it's where you grow. You could also say it's the *uncomfortable* zone. In this learning zone, or what Daniel Coyle calls the sweet spot, we are stretching just outside of our current capability and reaching for a target just beyond our grasp. It's not so far that success is unlikely, but far enough that is forces us to up our game a bit and push just a little harder. Much like strength training at the gym, it's when we force our muscles to lift just a little more weight than usual or push just one more rep that they become stronger.

In terms of skill building, this is the zone where our brain's neural connections are formed and strengthened. It is in this zone that deliberate practice yields the best results. This is where the magic happens and as your skill level increases, you want to continue to push the boundaries of your comfort zone by forcing yourself to keep training just beyond your current reach. Just remember, if it feels easy, then you're not there yet.

Finally - and of least value to us - beyond this learning zone is the breaking zone, and that is when we stretch so far beyond current capabilities that success is less than 20%, and probably just due to luck. In this zone, you are so far beyond your level of skill that you're generally overwhelmed and unlikely to make any gains. You need feedback and positive reinforcement to learn from your practice and you're unlikely to get that when in the breaking zone.

Emulate the Best – The process of learning new skills includes physical changes to your brain's neural connections and this can also be accomplished by watching others and through practicing with mental visualization. One of the best ways to start learning a new skill is by modeling those that are already great and emulating the things they do best. Identify those who have the skills you want and carefully watch them perform it. Study your role models and focus on the specifics to understand the intricacies of what they're doing and how they do it successfully. This has never been easier with today's age of readily accessible audio and video footage.

Visualization - Another way to ingrain a new skill is through visualization. The goal is to fill your mind with images of how the skill should be performed and then imagine yourself doing it. Pretend you are as good as your role model and "see yourself" performing the skill as they do. This is effective for both hard and soft skills. Chess players will train by replaying classic games move by move and expert salesmen will train through role-playing and responding to different situations and responses. Imagine yourself in a situation and visualize yourself making decisions and performing the skill just like your role model would.

Do it again and again and again – Let's face it, repetition is ultimately how a skill is developed and honed so we must learn to embrace the repetitiveness and practice as often as possible (but practice smart of course!) Learn to love the process and the results will begin to take care of themselves. Whether your aim is to develop elite physical skills or amazing mental abilities, you'll find that all of the highly skilled got there by putting themselves through incredible amounts of practice drills. It's not always fun and it's always hard work, but what they say is true: practice makes perfect. Even more important, practice make permanent!

"I fear not the man who has practiced 10,000 kicks once, but I fear the man who has practiced one kick 10,000 times."

– Bruce Lee

Top 10 Skills for Entrepreneurs

Here are a few essential skills that all entrepreneurs, sales professionals and business leaders should consider developing. (Bear in mind this is a small sampling

In no particular order:

1. Speed Reading – If you want to continue growing your knowledge base and improving your skills, then reading will play a significant role in that development. All leaders are avid readers and being able to read quickly and efficiently will pay enormous dividends in the long run.

2. Rapid Learning and Skill Acquisition – Yes, learning itself is a skill and understanding how to learn anything quickly and efficiently can put you miles ahead of the competition. Additionally, using techniques to develop an incredible memory will give you an edge. Use the techniques outlined in this chapter as well as those in the Knowledge chapter.

3. Public Speaking & Presentation – As an entrepreneur, you will often be presenting and explaining your ideas. This can include other forms of communication such as verbal and written communication.

4. Technical Skills – You probably shouldn't be the best programmer or graphic designer you know (unless that is your business), but having a basic level of technical skills will have tremendous benefits in today's highly technical world. Being able to quickly edit a web page, create a mock-up of an app, or query information in a database could give you just the edge you need. Additionally, since just about every business will now have some sort of technical aspect to it (web marketing, mobile apps, graphics, databases, etc.), having technical skills will also help you communicate with engineers and designers more effectively. This is also true for being able to review and understand financial spreadsheets and metrics.

5. Sales – Whether pitching your idea to potential investors and customers, or recruiting highly skilled people to work for your organization, having sales skills will be critical to your success. Even if you don't plan to work in a direct sales capacity, these skills are needed in almost all areas of life and should be developed.

6. Negotiation – Negotiation is something you use every day in both your business and personal life. Deal making is an integral part of business and negotiation will play a crucial role here. As an entrepreneur, this skill also goes far beyond just getting a better price or favorable terms: instead of wasting time arguing with others or trying to force people to do what you want, you can use negotiation skills to reach agreements, find win-win solutions, and keep you focused on the priorities.

7. Interpersonal Skills – Having good people skills is critical in life. This is just as important in business as it is with our family and friends. It's a skill we should all continue to improve on and you'll understand why after reading chapter six on Relationships.

8. Execution – Ideas are wonderful but they are worthless without effective implementation. Successful execution is what separates the winners from the losers. Admittedly, execution is a large group of skills, but there are few key sub-skills that generate high execution skills. This includes planning and project management, delegation, priority management, and problem solving just to name a few.

9. Leadership – Even if you plan on being a one-person business working from the comfort of your laptop, you must still

become a leader. Leadership is critical in all aspects of business, especially when building a new company.

10. Focus – Maintaining a laser-like focus on the ultimate goal and working on the task at hand without being distracted is a skill that we all need to develop. When trying to build a business there will be a seemingly endless list of distractions that have the potential to derail your progress. By nature, entrepreneurs are curious and prone to seeing new opportunities or better ideas everywhere. This skill is not easy to master, but is key to a successful future.

CHAPTER FIVE

Habits are the Key to Consistency

"We are what we repeatedly do. Excellence, therefore, is not an act, but a habit."

- Aristotle

One of the most challenging jobs in the world is being a CEO for a major corporation or startup. For most, this task consumes the person's life, requiring intense levels of sustained attention and energy. I marvel at how these individuals continue to perform at peak levels for so long. Then, I'm awestruck when I read about CEOs running not just one company, but successfully leading multiple businesses simultaneously. These are individuals such as Richard Branson, Elon Musk, and Jack Dorsey. What is their secret?

One common trait you'll find among the successful is that they always maintain great habits and routines. Whether that means waking up early for a morning routine of exercise and meditation or building the habit of goal setting, they all know that good habits create discipline and consistency. Benjamin Franklin was known for his focus on his self-improvement and he eventually published the strict daily routine that helped him manage his time. Professional athletes, CEOs, and even the President of the United States all have daily and weekly routines that help them maximize their waking hours and reach their goals.

Jack Dorsey, the CEO of Square and Founder of Twitter, gave some insights during an interview about juggling the workload required to lead both companies. Dorsey said, "The only way to do this is to be very disciplined and very practiced." He was referring to his routine for managing both businesses. To stay focused and productive, he established a weekly routine that "themes his days" so that he can focus on just one area of the business each weekday. For example, Tuesdays are for Product Development. Wednesdays for Marketing, Communications & Growth. Saturdays he takes off to go hiking and Sundays are for reflections, feedback and to set the strategy for the upcoming week. As Dorsey put it, "There is interruption all the time but I can quickly deal with an interruption and then know that it's Tuesday, I have product meetings and I need to focus on product stuff." He said, "This also sets a good cadence for the rest of the company."

Jack Dorsey understands the power of having solid routines and strong habits and he uses them to also drive the culture in his companies. Creating a routine around his week has allowed Dorsey and his leadership team to stay disciplined and productive for 16 hours a day as they lead two vast and public companies.

How Habits Fit into SHARK Belief

The H in SHARK Belief stands for Habits. This refers to everything we call habits, routines, or rituals. This can be a habit we do automatically as a result of some trigger or it can represent a routine we've disciplined ourselves to maintain as we progress toward a particular goal. Habits are critical to success because of their cumulative effect over time. Their power comes from consistency. Habits also harmonize with other elements of SHARK Belief such as the Skills element and our Beliefs. For example, if you have determined that one of the skills you need to develop is computer programming, then a routine to drive you to practice regularly will help build that skill. Remember that developing skill is about learning through repetitive practice and it's your habits and routines that will get you there. What types of habits or routines would you need to develop to reach your goals? If you had to pick just one habit, which would it be? Keep this in mind as you go through this chapter. I will show you some habit hacks to help you get started.

Studies have shown that a large percent of our daily activity and thoughts are really just habits in action. Some studies show it to be around 45% of our activity and others argue it's closer to 90%. They say that about 90% of the activities you did today were done in the same way as yesterday and the day before that and so on. It's the same with our thought patterns, they are generally the same day in and day out. Since habits drive most of our daily actions and it's our actions that ultimately determine our level of success, it's critical that we develop habits of success.

In Charles Duhigg's book *The Power of Habit*, he gives many examples of how habits drive all aspects of human behavior and interaction. Not only do they drive our personal activity, but they influence group behavior as well, from football teams to world-class companies. In his book, he shares the story of Tony Dungy's methods of changing the football players' habits on the field, which allowed them to respond instinctively and ultimately led the team to a Super Bowl Championship! By changing the player's habits, they were able to react to cues from their opponents instead of relying on real-time decision making during each play of the game. This gave his team an edge over other teams because those split seconds made the difference between winning and losing a game. All successful people and organizations have good habits that have helped them get to where they are. They also have good success habits to keep them moving forward.

Good Intentions Are Not Enough

Has the following scenario ever happened to you? You attended a seminar and come away with a lot of useful tips for achieving personal growth and success. One speaker shares some good ideas that you write down. Then another speaker lays out several more. You take plenty of good notes and soon you have a ton of ideas and action plans. You are motivated to implement some of those ideas right away, so you pick a few to start working on. Then, after only a couple of weeks, you find that you aren't doing everything you needed to do each day. You had good intentions but after a long day of work or because of unexpected events, you can never seem to find the time or the energy, so those new routines and ideas get pushed aside.

This would happen to me all the time and I never could figure out what I was doing wrong. I would get highly motivated but could never seem to keep the momentum. Then to make matters worse, I would hear about a successful person that somehow had time to run multiple businesses, exercise daily, enjoy some recreational hobbies, publish a few books along the way and even spend quality time with their families? How do they do it?! I mean we all have the same 24 hours in a day right? I would often find myself saying, "They are a machine!" For many people, the new ideas and actions are just not high enough on the priority list and it's not really an issue of having time or energy. For others, it's simple a matter of organization. Either way, good intentions are never enough.

After learning from the leaders of personal development such as Tony Robbins and Brian Tracy, I finally realized one of their secrets of success: good habits. With the good habits they had developed over time, they could maximize their productivity while using the same amount of mental energy and time as everyone else! Sure, all successful people are hard workers also. In fact, they work harder than most, but it's their habits and routines that combine hard work with consistency and discipline. A lot of people work hard but they aren't all successful. That is because success requires that you work hard and smart. Don't just expend energy to feel like you're giving it your all. You've got to put in a disciplined and deliberate effort to see the results you want. Do everything for a reason and with consistency, and over time you will begin to see results.

I'll get into some particular success habits and tips you can use to do the same but the point is that good habits and routines are paramount to your success. You can't always count on your levels of motivation to carry you through the tough times. Emotions are fickle and you will not feel inspired and excited every day. Also, your willpower is finite. It will help you in the short run and can get you started, but until you build up that willpower muscle, you need habits and routines to keep you disciplined and moving forward.

You can tell a lot about a person's habits by looking at their life. You can probably guess a person's exercise and dietary habits by their appearance. Their spending will reflect financial habits and their thought habits will influence how they speak and act. Some people are habitually negative and pessimistic to the point where it's the first reaction to just about everything. Others are habitually positive and see opportunity everywhere. It becomes an automatic response.

Habits permeate so much of our lives that we must recognize and influence them, otherwise we'll never have a shot at successfully acting on the other elements of SHARK Belief, or, for that matter, reaching our goals. We are all slaves to habits, so it's up to us to be slaves to the right habits. This is about designing a life and aiming for success. Think of good habits as the foundation that you will build on. They will drive consistency and progress which are both necessary for reaching any goal. I will lay out some ideas for habits and routines that you should consider adopting. To stay on top of latest the hacks, visit SHARKBelief.com, where I keep an updated list and always post new articles, habit hacks, and recommended books to help you succeed in this area.

Habits vs. Routines & Rituals

When I use the terms habits, it has a slightly different meaning than when I say routines and rituals. With habits, I am referring to actions that drive character and personal development. This could represent habits such as goal setting, exercise, prayer, or meditation. While these may not be directly related to your goal, you'll find that they will still influence your level of success.

Routines are often externally focused and support professional development. Setting up an automatic schedule of productivity actions, routines, and rituals will help drive discipline. Examples include practicing your programming skills, making sales calls, networking, or regular writing towards a book project.

There is a slight overlap in that some habits will benefit you both personally and professionally. For example, getting up early to execute a morning routine is a big habit that also serves as a trigger for action towards other habits that can be either personal or professional or a mixture of both. I have established the habit of getting up a little bit earlier than I used to so that I can go through a morning routine. During this time, I will act on other habits I've developed such as prayer, reading, and reviewing my goals and actions for the day.

Willpower

There have been dozens of studies on willpower over the years with one of the most famous being the Stanford marshmallow experiment conducted by Walter Mischel in the late 1960's. In this study, they sat four-year-olds in front of a marshmallow and told the children that if they could wait ten minutes and not eat the marshmallow, they would be given a second marshmallow. Most of the four-year-olds could not resist that yummy-looking marshmallow in front of them, and so chose to have a single marshmallow right then rather than wait ten minutes and have two marshmallows. The study didn't end there. What researchers found was that the children who exhibited stronger willpower were also the ones who went on to achieve higher academic performances, were most likely to be popular with their peers and ultimately gained admission into better universities.

Studies have shown that willpower (or self-discipline) has a bigger effect on academic performance than intellectual talent. In other words, self-discipline is a higher predictor of success than IQ! I realized this years ago when I began to notice that some of my friends, who were brilliant and accomplished academically, could not seem to find any level of success in the real world. They could not find or hold a job, they generally didn't exercise and seemed to always have trouble in their relationships. It became apparent that it takes more than just brains to be successful. Knowledge is essential but you also need self-discipline. If all it required were a big IQ, then all of our schools would be filled with billionaire professors.

So then, why doesn't everyone just use their self-discipline and willpower to reach the level of success they want? Well, the problem is that daily willpower is finite. Think of it as a muscle or the energy in a battery. When you first wake up in the morning, you have a full charge for the day and your willpower is the strongest at that time. However, as you make decisions throughout the day and take actions, you begin to "use up" your willpower. My personal level usually hits a low point around 2PM. After a break or some coffee and food, I get a second burst and the levels go back up to carry me through the evening. However, it's certainly not as strong as when I first get up in the morning.

The good news is that since willpower is like a muscle, it can be strengthened. Think of it as a skill that can be learned and improved over time. We can learn to regulate our impulses and distract ourselves from temptations. However, until we can get our self-discipline to the level where we always take consistent action, we need a way to bypass it when willpower and motivation levels are low. How is that done? You guessed it... through habits and rituals. The best way to manage your finite willpower energy is to create a habit or routine. Often times, when someone exhibits great willpower, it may just be a good habit that has since become automatic and is driving the discipline. Very little willpower is needed once a habit is established.

Habit Hacks – How to Start & Sustain New Habits & Rituals

Mini Habits

In his book *Mini Habits*, Stephen Guise does an excellent job explaining willpower and how to maximize it with mini habits. A good way to start building a new habit is to use your willpower to create a mini habit, which builds momentum and eventually grows into the full blown habit you wish to develop. A mini habit is a small and positive behavior that you force yourself to do every day. As Guise puts it, it's "too small to fail" nature makes it weightless, deceptively powerful, and a superior habit-building strategy.

Let's say you want to build a habit of going to the gym five days a week. Just the thought of it can drain your willpower. Instead, set your goal to one push-up a day. Just one! It's so small and seemingly insignificant that it would be almost impossible to fail. What ends up happening is that once you're in the push-up stance, you'll likely do more than just one push-up. One turns into several, and eventually you build up to exercising several days a week. It's a great way to break inertia and get started. Also, sticking to this mini habit is physiologically rewarding, which generates more motivation. Even on your off days, you could still do just one push-up and keep your string of wins going.

As Stephen Guise states, "mini habits are designed for minimum willpower exertion and maximum momentum – the perfect scenario." We have to be smart about how we managed our willpower energy each day, and the best way to use this finite resource is to use it towards building a new habit or routine. The eventual result will be an automatic and subconscious behavior that can overcome our down days when motivation is low and fatigue has set in. Since our brain resists significant changes, a mini habit is an awesome way to get started and will conserve your willpower strength.

There has been plenty of research to show how critical small wins are to our ultimate success. We all need immediate feedback to help us believe we can succeed, which in turn inspires us to persist and do more. Frequent small wins positively influence your mindset and boost your confidence and motivation.

Professional coaches often use this technique when they see one of their athletes start to falter. Instead of going for a big pass or the home run, they'll aim for just a couple of yards, or a single-base hit. These small successes let the team experience a small bit of victory, which then builds momentum and changes the trajectory of the team's performance. While I'm a big believer in dreaming big, it's the small wins and frequent rewards that keep us going. Our mental state and beliefs are the secret sauce that brings together the SHARK Belief elements, so these frequent wins are essential. Just like quitting and giving up too soon can become habitual for the non-successful person, you can just as easily form the habit of winning.

Consistency is the Power Behind Habits & Routines

When I was working in real estate, I studied under the great real estate sales teacher Brian Buffini. He taught a simple routine of daily activities that would generate sales from referrals. The magic in this routine was not a groundbreaking idea that would produce results after a single day of doing it. No, the magic was in the compounding effect of doing it day in and day out! The motto was "Win the Day!" By focusing on just one day and doing what needs to be done, the long run will take care of itself. Anyone who has studied finance knows how powerful this is: a couple hundred dollars consistently invested per month turns into millions over time through compounding.

This same effect is true with our personal development and through our daily habits. As Brian Buffini often said, "Win enough days, and you will win the week. Win enough weeks and you will win the month. Win enough months, and you will win the year!" Just imagine how awesome a year you would have with a few simple habits implemented over the course of months. Time flies and it's going to pass anyway. A few months or a year may seem like a long time from now, but when you get there, it'll feel sudden. If you haven't accomplished any goals, you'll wonder where the time went. Today is the day of action and there's no better action to take than an activity that will build on itself and move you in the direction of your goal. There is room for "off days" and it doesn't require absolute perfection. We're all human right? However, minimize the off-days as much as possible. Doing something for six days out of seven, for months on end will yield tremendous results. You can achieve the extraordinary, by doing the ordinary, *consistently*!

Part of consistency is timing. We need to perform the new habit or routine at a consistent time of day for it to take hold. This is especially important early on since you will generally never "find time" to do it. You need to schedule it in and be deliberate about making it happen. There are two ways to do this. The first is basically scheduling it for a particular time of the day. This is easiest for those who have a relatively set schedule and can count on being able to do their habit or routine at regular time of day. The second method is for those who need a little more flexibility, but can still count on some regular event to kick off the routine. For example, doing your habit when you first wake up or after finishing lunch.

HABITS ARE THE KEY TO CONSISTENCY

While you may not always go to sleep at the same time or get home from work at 5pm every day, you can still make your habit trigger relative to some other event, regardless of what time of the day it is. Doing this will maintain consistency and help solidify the new routine.

Another good hack is what I call habit chaining. This involves "linking" a new habit to be triggered by your current habit. A simple example would be flossing. If you wanted to start flossing once a day, it's easy to link this new habit to your current habit of brushing your teeth. Of course, the linked habits do not have to relate, it's just a good reference point that makes starting the new habit easier. Because you're already in a sort of 'auto-pilot mode,' the willpower factor is not an issue. To take advantage of this technique, think of routines or recurring actions you already take and try linking a new habit to one of those.

Keep an eye on the goal and pick your habits carefully. Be deliberate about which habit or routine you implement, and understand how it will help you. This is important because you will not always feel that emotional high every time you think about your goal. There will be days when your motivation levels are low and the only thing you want to do is sit on the couch with a fresh pizza and binge watch all five seasons of your favorite TV show. However, if you begin to focus on the process and learn to enjoy it, you will be able to look back one day and see how far you've come. Build momentum and keep momentum. The results will be extraordinary because of the cumulative effect of ordinary action repeatedly done over time.

Your Brain Loves Habits

Let's take a quick look at the science of your mind and why it needs habits. Though just a few pounds in weight, your brain will consume an incredible 25% of your body's total energy each day. Your brain uses more energy than any other single system in your body. Thus, your brain needs to find ways to be as efficient as possible, and it does so by adapting. You make thousands of decisions on a given day and most of those are done very quickly and usually subconsciously. Your brain develops habits and thought patterns so that it can put you on a kind of autopilot, which then allows your brain to conserve energy. This energy can be used for making more important decisions and learning.

Our brain is an amazing machine that is always seeking ways to become more efficient. It essentially reprograms itself by forming habits. Imagine the path of water flowing down a hill for the first time. At first, it may just find the several random groves to spread across as it makes its way down. However, as the water continues to flow, it deepens a groove with each passing. The path the water takes starts to solidify and eventually forms a very clear and distinct path as it flows down the hill. Over time, this is how streams and creeks are carved. Once there, the water will likely never take another path unless there is something new to force the change.

Likewise, our brain forms and strengthens neurological connections every time we repeat a task. This neurological "pathway" is strengthened so that our brain has a solid route to quickly and easily send a signal. Any repeated task eventually becomes habitual as our minds adjust to perform automatically. Initially, that thought pattern takes a lot of mental energy, but over time, it becomes so efficient that it uses the same level of brain energy that is used when sleeping.

When I first learned to drive, I paid careful attention to a multitude of things going on around me, making a ton of decisions real-time. I was watching the cars move all around me, reacting to the traffic signals, braking, accelerating, turning, checking the mirrors and so on. It was exhausting at first! After a few weeks of doing my best to not run anyone over or hit parked cars, driving started to become really easy.

Fast forward to today and now my driving habits are almost subconscious. When I see the brake lights of the car in front of me, it takes but a split second for me to lift my foot off the gas pedal and prepare to stop. I've been "trained" to respond to the cue of brake lights, and that's a good thing because it keeps me safe. Driving has become so automatic that in addition to driving, I can now have a conversation, sing along to the radio, and dare I say, even check my phone… all at the same time! Okay, maybe in my younger days but now I really do put safety first. Here's my public service announcement… Please don't text while driving; I've got a baby on board!

Anatomy of a Habit

There are three essential components to a habit. Understanding them will help you to better create and control them. First is the cue, which is some event or action that triggers the habitual behavior. Second is the actual behavior or routine. And finally, there is the all-important reward. Triggers and rewards may be difficult to identify, but all habits are reinforced and ultimately solidified because there is a reward or some satisfaction that comes from doing the behavior. This is true for both good and bad habits. Once you learn to structure a habit into its three components, it becomes easier to either build new healthy habits or to modify an existing one by understanding what the triggers are and the reward your brain is craving.

There is a law of habits that states, "a habit cannot be eliminated." Rather, you merely modify the habitual behavior or routine. The cue and the reward (or its equivalent) stay the same but the routine action in between is what has actually changed. It's funny, our brain is so efficient and amazing yet it hates sudden changes and often works against us by resisting change. A good way to hack this is to either make the change gradual or trick the brain by keeping the trigger and reward while changing the routine.

New Habits Form in Days; or is it Weeks or maybe Months...

There is a lot of research and debate around the ideal length of time it will take to develop a new habit. Some say it takes 21-30 days while others say it can be done in as little as a week. Still others claim it takes more than six months. The truth is that it will vary from person to person and will depend on things such as how big a change the new habit will create and how often the new activity is done. You can build or modify a new habit much quicker if it's an activity you do several times a day versus something you do only once a day or few times a week. The key is repetition so the more often and consistently a new activity is done, the sooner it will become a habit. Another factor is the time and energy required for the new routine. It will be a lot easier to develop the habit of flossing your teeth once a day than it will be to develop the habit of exercising for 30 minutes every day. However, there are some hacks to get around this such as starting with a mini habit.

Creating a new habit will almost always take longer than you think and it will likely be harder than you realize. You must commit to sticking with it for much longer than you think it will take to form a habit if you're serious about making the necessary changes in your life. If you think it will take 30 days, then commit to 90 before evaluating or changing course. Your current habits have been in place for years, maybe even decades, and they will take longer than you think to change. However, the time it takes to change them will be a blip in time compared to how long you've been doing your current habits. It's like turning a massive battleship. Doesn't happen fast, but once it starts on a new course, it begins to build huge momentum! I often hear people say "but I've tried that and it didn't work for me"…then I'll ask "how long did you try it?" The reply is often, "I gave it a few days or a couple of weeks." Listen, if you're going to do something life-changing, you need to give it more than just a few weeks or even a few months! Commit to something for the long haul. Many people lack persistence because they have formed the habit of quitting too soon and this habit has been reinforced by the rewards of temporary comfort and the lure of the next new thing. Don't give up on a new routine too soon. Develop the habit of persistence and give it time to work.

Keystone Habits

Okay, so you now know how important habits are and even how to start them. You probably can think of several new habits you'd like to instill in your daily routine. But remember, we cannot overwhelm our brain with too many changes all at once or it will be impossible to stick with any of them. The answer then is deciding which one or two habits are the most important or powerful of the group. In Charles Duhigg's book *The Power of Habit*, he introduces the concept of keystone habits. These are key habits that have the power to start a chain reaction, which will then make changing other habits easier as the positive effects spread to other areas of your life and daily patterns. The point is that some habits matter more than others, so we want to start with those. These Keystone habits have the power to cause widespread shifts in seemingly unrelated areas.

For example, studies show that people who begin exercising will suddenly change their eating habits and become more productive at work. They smoke less and show more patience with colleagues and friends. Another example of a keystone habit for some people is making the bed every morning. This is correlated with better productivity and a greater sense of well-being, which then begins to impact the habit of sticking with a budget. It's not that making your bed causes you to spend money more wisely, but rather the mind-shift resulting from the keystone habit helps other good habits to take hold.

Habit Collecting

To become a success machine, your quest should be to instill many successful habits and routines. However, don't try to build ten new habits all at once. Focus on just one or maybe two at the most. Remember, the brain resists change, so it can be very hard to implement too many changes all at once. While you may find yourself suddenly making changes to several other areas of your life due to the effects of keystone habits, it should never be your plan going in.

If you try to simultaneously start the habit of daily prayer, regular exercising, reading ten pages a day and making ten sales calls a day, you will never be able to stick with it all. While it is entirely possible to build yourself up to doing all of those things and much more each day, you have to gradually introduce one new habit at a time. Trying to stick to several habits at once will be a major drain on your willpower and energy, which increases the likelihood of failure. This failure, in turn, keeps you from experiencing those much-needed wins resulting in lower motivation and soon it becomes a downward spiral. It's a paradox but to go fast, you first have to go slow.

This is the idea behind habit collecting. Some people spend a lot of time collecting rare books, movies or even rocks. Don't laugh, I used to collect rocks as a kid! We should all become collectors of awe-inspiring success habits. Focus your time and energy on building and mastering just one habit at a time. Then, when your routine becomes easy and almost automatic, you'll be ready to move on to the next one. In just a short time, you'll be surprised at your impressive and growing collection of good habits. Just like goals, you will be more successful by narrowing your focus to just one or two at a time. What you will find is that many habits synergize with other habits making it even easier to add new ones over time.

Top Ten Success Habits

Here is a brief list of ideas and general habits to help you get started. Keep in mind that you will need to establish habits or routines that are specific to your goal, but these habits are common among the ultra-successful and they should be considered part of your daily routine.

1. Daily Goal Writing – As noted in the Aim chapter, setting a clear goal is critical to success as goals give us focus and clarity about what we want to achieve. However, most people don't review those goals regularly. In his book *The 10X Rule*, Grant Cardone shares that he doesn't just write his goals once and then forget about them. Instead, he writes his goals down

twice a day, every day! First thing in the morning and just before bed. Other writers such as Earl Nightingale have also suggested reviewing our goals daily. Whether it's writing them down or just reading them out loud, reviewing your goals every day will keep you focused on where you are going and what you need to do. It's about mindfulness.

2. Visualization – Used by successful athletes, keynote speakers, and entrepreneurs, regular visualization is key to keeping you on track with your bigger vision. I talk more about visualization in the Beliefs chapter but it's important to realize that most successful people do this in some fashion.

3. Maintain a To-Do List – All successful people have a list of priorities and things they need to get done. This is best done *the night before* your day begins. Prioritize the night before. You'll not only sleep better, but also start your day off with purpose and direction. Don't put too much on the list but always list at least one important thing that needs to be done that day. This habit will increase your productivity by leaps and bounds and will also give you that sense of accomplishment every day.

4. Wake Up Early – Create the habit of waking up early. It's a great way to link on new habits by creating a morning routine. Hal Alrod wrote an excellent book on this topic called *The Miracle Morning*. It's an easy read that is packed with great tips and reasons why we can all benefit from a Miracle Morning Routine.

5. Read Every Day – Never stop learning and gaining more knowledge about what you aim to achieve. Research from Tom Corley showed that 88% of the wealthy read 30 minutes

or more each day for education or career reasons vs. 2% of the poor. It's a critical habit to develop no matter what your goal is. You don't have to start with 30 minutes, but read every day, even if it's just a few minutes.

6. Exercise – It's not news to anyone that exercise is critical. Most of us want to do more but usually don't make time for it. Exercise is more than just losing weight and looking fit. It's about living a healthy and full life. It keeps our minds sharp, improves our emotional well-being and all-around quality of life. Make it a habit.

7. Prayer or Meditation – There are many studies to show the tremendous benefits to prayer and meditation. Even if you're not a spiritual or religious person, you can benefit from clearing the mind and relaxing for a few minutes each day. You'll find this habit among some of the most famous and successful people today.

8. Networking & Relationship Building – All successful people make time to regularly meet new people or connect with those who help them move towards their goals. It doesn't matter what your goal is, you will always need some sort of relationship with others to help you get there. Whether it's a coach, mentor, or accountability partner, certain people can help us reach our goals. As discussed extensively in the Relationships Chapter, our network and relationships will determine the level of success we achieve in life. Make meeting new people or staying in touch a strong habit.

9. Skills Development – Your goal will likely require that you develop certain skills or techniques. The best way to do this is by practicing and learning, and the best way to make sure

you're doing those two things is by creating a routine that supports them. Schedule time to practice regularly and develop your skills. All successful people are highly skilled and that did not happen by accident. They made time to develop those skills and you can do that by creating a habit around them.

10. Giving – Whether it's regularly volunteering or giving to your favorite charity or local church, habitual giving is one of those habits that helps us in many ways. Tony Robbins says we are happiest when we are growing or giving. You'll find that nearly all successful and wealthy people are also big givers. Don't wait until you have more to give. Start now with what you know and with what you have and make giving a habit.

Key Points to Remember:

Start Small – Start with a habit smaller than what you ultimately want to build up to. If your goal is to make ten sales calls a day, then start with making just one call a day. If you decide to make more than one call, great! The key is to never make less than one call, or five calls, or whatever your mini habit is. Build that habit by starting small. Make it easy to win, and the wins will keep you going.

One at a Time – Focus on creating or modifying one habit at a time. Once you get the hang of it, you can bump that up to two or three, but never try to make many changes all at once. Remember, our brain strives to be efficient and will resist too much change all at once. The goal is to build the routine to the point where it becomes automatic and easy. Save your willpower for building up one strong habit.

Consistency – Remember, it's the cumulative effect that makes habits stick. One way to make it easier is to have a regular time for doing the new habit. This can be either a set time of the day or it can be relative to some other event such as waking up or getting home from work. Once it's a solid habit or routine, varying the time will be a little easier to sustain. Consistency is key.

100% commitment – You cannot be 80% or 90% or even 99% committed to your goal. You have to be 100% committed no matter what! Never miss a time period – even if you do it partially, you need to keep momentum by doing something. The biggest habit-buster is missing two or more consecutive routine cycles. Do this a few times and you should just start over to get a fresh start. Remember that building a new habit will probably take longer than you anticipate, so make the commitment ahead of time that you are going to stick with it, especially when it becomes difficult to do.

For more on how to build killer habits or for my recommended list of top habit books, go to SHARKBelief.com.

CHAPTER SIX

Good Relationships Breed Success

"Individually, we are one drop. Together, we are an ocean."

- Ryunosuke Satoro

In 2014, Tom Brady led the New England Patriots as they marched through the playoffs and ultimately defeated the Seattle Seahawks to win the Super Bowl Championship. It was another highly controversial season for Brady and his team but this win gave Brady his fourth Super Bowl ring, tying him with Joe Montana and Terry Bradshaw for most Super Bowl victories by a starting quarterback. It also gave Brady his third Super Bowl MVP award and he was soon being listed as one of the greatest quarterbacks to ever play the game. He has led his team to six Super Bowls, winning four of them. He also won the league MVP award twice and has been elected to the Pro Bowl eleven times. Tom Brady has led the Patriots to more division titles than any other quarterback in NFL history and also helped set the record for most consecutive playoff wins.

GOOD RELATIONSHIPS BREED SUCCESS

In spite of the controversy surrounding Tom Brady and the New England Patriots' methods of winning, there is no doubt that Brady is an incredibly skilled quarterback and should be ranked among the best to ever play. My point, however, is not make a case for Tom Brady being the best quarterback ever because everyone knows that title belongs to Joe Montana. My point is that even with his remarkable skills, Tom Brady would not have been able to achieve all that he has without his team and without the support of countless other individuals. All professional American football teams depend on the various skills and effort from each of the players. Each player on the field has an entirely different role and you cannot just replace one with the other. Although it would be fantastically entertaining, you'll never see a 450-pound lineman switching places with an agile wide receiver. They each play a different role and have a particular purpose on the team. Beyond just the players, a typical professional football team will also have a staff that runs into the hundreds of people.

In the same regard, Tom Brady and his team also depend on the leadership of their coaches and trainers. They depend on the support staff, the strategic experts in the booth and even the fans and cheerleaders. Everyone from the business and marketing teams to the locker-room ball handlers all plays a role in helping Brady and the Patriots win enough games to be crowned Super Bowl Champions. As great a quarterback as Tom Brady has been, he would not have been able to beat even a high school football team if it were just him on the field. While he is ultimately the one making the split-second decisions and throwing the ball downfield, any quarterback still needs his team and his coach to be successful. As this relates to your own personal success, you also need others to help you reach the pinnacles of success. As the quarterback of your own life, you are still the one that needs to make the final decisions and take action. However, a team of key relationships, partners and coaches will help you get there.

Relationships & Success

In terms of SHARK Belief, the R is for Relationships and describes the people we need in our lives to help us achieve our goals. Just as important, we must also be mindful of toxic relationships and know which people to avoid. We've all heard that old cliché, "It's not what you know, but *who* you know that matters." Have you ever stopped to consider why it matters? We've heard it so much that most of us have internalized it and will even repeat it as a way to justify the success stories of others. When we hear of a famous actor or business professional getting their start after meeting just the right person, we're quick to say, "See, it's all about who you know." It's the classic right place at the right time scenario and we'll either credit that person's connections for their success or we'll give the credit to good luck.

By now, you have learned that achieving success certainly requires more than just knowing the right people or having powerful connections. However, there is no denying that our relations are integral to the level of success we achieve in life. This is one of the reasons professional networking organizations and websites like LinkedIn or MeetUp have had such massive success. Business professionals understand the power of one's network and most people, in general, want to connect with other like-minded people.

Successful business leaders and professionals understand the value of relationships and they are strategic about networking and leveraging their contacts to reach their goals. They always have coaches, advisors, and mentors on their side and they understand that they cannot do it all by themselves and will collaborate with others to share ideas, motivate each other and to brainstorm solutions. You'll notice that all successful people have a team supporting them in their efforts. Regardless of how big or small your goals are, you also need a team and should begin connecting with others. Meeting new people has never been easier than in today's ultra-connected world.

For the entrepreneur, this is critical because there isn't a single business in the world that can succeed without other people. Beyond your customers, you'll need to work with many other people to help you accomplish your goals including partners, investors, mentors and suppliers. For anyone looking to build an organization, the definition itself implies that you will be leading or coordinating with other people. Perhaps most importantly, working with other persons can bridge a gap in skills or knowledge that you may not possess but need for your goal. If you are an entrepreneur, it may benefit you to hire or partner with someone that has the skills or knowledge you need. This could include technical skills such as programming or business skills such as marketing and sales. By now you know how essential skills and knowledge are to your success and working with others is the quickest way to bridge a gap in these areas.

Another important reason to connect with others is to help you get started. If you have a goal but are not sure how to get started, connecting with someone already doing what you want to do is the best way to go. This will significantly shorten your learning curve and you'll also benefit from learning what NOT to do which can help you avoid costly mistakes. In today's highly connected world, it's dangerous to take a "me against the world" mentality. Even the extreme introvert, hermit or web-only guy will eventually need to develop some fundamental relationships to reach the next level of their success.

As John Donne famously wrote, "No man is an island, entire of itself, every man is a piece of the continent, a part of the main." Life is about relationships and we as a part of humanity are all interconnected. This is especially true for anyone looking to achieve great things or create new organizations. Your personal interactions with your network of friends and family, coworkers, mentors, teammates and even your competitors will ultimately paint a reflection of who you are or who you will become. Your personal interactions create your life's environment and experiences.

Relationships are crucial to success not because of what "we can get" from the other person or because others can help us with something we need, but more importantly, relationships are important because they are a constant exchange of influence, ideas, mindset, and information between those involved. It's more than just surrounding yourself with certain people because they can help you get the deal done. It's about surrounding yourself with other people because of how they think!

We become like those we associate with and our relationships will have a tremendous influence on whom we become. If your closest relationships are in direct opposition to your goals and aspirations, then you will be in a constant uphill battle and likely meet with failure before you see success. Success begins in the mind and you need to be on guard from the negative influences of your associates. If your three closest friends are always depressed, broke and angry, then guess what? You'll be the fourth. If your three closest friends are driven, optimistic and successful, then guess what? You'll be the fourth. Be careful not to spend too much time with those that are constantly negative, pessimistic and angry, or you'll have a hard time keeping the success mentality required to persevere and reach your goals.

Napoleon Hill often spoke of the Mastermind Principle and the synergistic effects of two or more minds working together in a spirit of harmony towards a single purpose. This harmonious alliance of two or more minds is more than what sociologists refer to as 'group think', but rather this meeting of the minds creates a new and separate 'blended mind' through which the group's individuals can tap into the knowledge, ideas, and creativity they could not have otherwise accessed alone. It is often this sharing of ideas and information that brings forth incredible accomplishments.

Imagine if Steve Jobs had never met Steve Wozniak or if Sergey Brin and Larry Page had decided not to work together on indexing the world's information? Would Apple and Google have ever existed and even if they had, would they have been able to accomplish the things that have changed our world? These are extreme examples but the point is the same. Who we connect with and the relationships we cultivate will ultimately shape our experiences and create the world in which we live.

As a child, my mom was always interested in who my friends were because she knew how much influence they would have on me. She, like all good parents, did her best to keep me away from those bad influences that could get me into trouble. In all of our relationships, we are either being influenced or we are influencing others. With this in mind, you should always guard your thoughts from destructive negative opinions and toxic emotions. This also means that you'll have to stop associating with certain people or do your best to limit time with them. If some people are always pulling you down or influencing you to engage in behavior destructive to your goals and potential, then why continue to subject yourself to it? It's not always easy, but you should reflect from time to time and examine your personal relationships through this lens.

Are there people in your life that are always criticizing your ideas and dreams? Do they try to impose their own limiting beliefs onto you? Are you being influenced to conform to the standards of low achievers? Are you being told to settle and just be happy with what you have? Unfortunately, the answer to these questions is yes for too many people. If you also answered yes to many of these questions, then it may be time for you to identify the people that you need to begin limiting time with. It may also be time to find some new friends or coworkers. Which would have a greater impact on your confidence and success, hanging around people that say it can't be done or being around people that encourage you and keep you motivated? How much more could you do if you regularly associated with optimistic and ambitious individuals that also wanted to see you succeed and lifted you up during setbacks? The good news is, they are out there and they want to connect with you also.

Make a deliberate effort to seek out and connect with the ambitious, optimistic and the success-minded. Constantly seek to connect with those pursuing similar goals. You are not going to just 'happen to meet them' but rather, you'll have to put energy into establishing these relationships. However long it takes, it will be worth it! Regardless of the goals you've set for yourself, there are some fundamental relationships everyone should have to maximize successful thinking and action. From wise counselors to accountability partners and even our followers, there are many relationships we need in our lives if we are to be truly successful in life. More specifically, there are four must-have relationships necessary for anyone that is serious about achieving massive success. I cover these in detail later but they are mentors, coaches, mastermind groups and mentees.

It is our relationships that often bring the most joy and happiness into our lives and make our endeavors that much more fulfilling. Remember, the journey truly is the reward and it is in our relationships that we find the most riches. Apart from your mindset, nothing will have more of an impact on your success and happiness than the quality and quantity of your relationships. It's about going further with more people rather than going faster all alone.

You Are the Average of Your Five Closest Friends

"You are the average of the five people you associate with most, so do not underestimate the effects of your pessimistic, unambitious, or disorganized friends. If someone isn't making you stronger, they're making you weaker."

— *Tim Ferriss*

Think about the five closest people you spend the most time with. Outside of your immediate family, who are your five closest friends? Who do you communicate with most often? Who are the 5 people that you interact with most at work or school? Once you've determined who these five people are, do a quick assessment of their finances, their health, their attitudes and their outlook on life. Are they positive or are they constantly negative and complaining? Are they healthy and full of energy or overweight and lethargic? Do they have dreams and goals? Are they holding themselves to a higher standard and expecting more than just average lives? Do they read personal development books or attend seminars? Are they always learning new skills and gaining knowledge? Do they have an entrepreneurial and success oriented mindset?

If it was not easy to yes to most of these questions, then you have to seriously consider the people you're spending the majority of your time with and begin looking to add new relationships to your life. It's not about being "too good" for the people in your life. It's not about being self-righteous or seeing yourself as superior to your friends and family. I'm not telling you to cut off your closest relationships if they don't align with your goals and aspirations. I'm certainly not saying that you should weigh every new relationship based on its economic potential. However, I am asking you to seriously consider whether or not your five closest friends are holding you back through their negative influences. Even common complacency rubs off on you and subtly begins to tell you that it's okay to not work so hard, to relax and accept being average. It's easy to get caught up with the "I hate Mondays" and "TGIF" crowd. Here's something people often forget: You have a choice on who you spend time with. Maybe it's time for a change.

While difficult at first, it is sometimes necessary to begin limiting the time you spend with old friends. If your high school buddies are still doing the same thing ten years later, it's time to get some new friends. If you're the smartest person in your group, then maybe it's time you get a new group. If you're the most successful or the most ambitious person in your group, then you definitely need to get a new group. If you're the healthiest, the most fit person in your group, be on guard because it will only be a matter of time before those with a lower standard begin to influence you to lower your own. You are fooling yourself if you believe that the people you most associate with have no influence on your thoughts and actions. This is especially important when it comes to achieving your goals. Who you spend time with influences the person you ultimately come, so by choosing whom those people will be, you are literally shaping your own future. This is the point Jim Rohn was making when he said, *"You are the average of the five people you spend the most time with."*

It goes beyond just limiting time with friends that have a negative influence or pessimistic outlooks. It also means we need to be deliberate about associating with those that push us and make us better. If your goal is to be a successful entrepreneur, then you should regularly be spending time with other entrepreneurs and those that have already been successful in business. If your goal is to stick to an exercise routine and lose weight, then find others that are also physically active and diet-conscious. There is a reason millionaires prefer to hang around other millionaires and billionaires with other billionaires. You'll see this in every social circle including age groups, religious groups or political parties. It's about aligning with others you can relate to and learn from.

Will every single one of our relationships be fully aligned with our beliefs, goals, and dreams? Of course not. Sometimes you are the one others will look up to and want to be like. Sometimes you're the one teaching others. Sometimes you're the one to open a door of opportunity for someone that can do nothing for you in return. Associating with people different from ourselves will add spice to life, introduces us to new ideas and perhaps do nothing more than teach us some much needed patience.

People can take this concept to an extreme and believe that they must have nothing to do with others that are not success-driven, wealthy or influential. Approaching relationships based on what they can do for you is snobbish, judgmental and disingenuous. Don't be that person! Be generous, serve other people and make real connections. Be authentic in your relationships and take an honest interest in other persons. This is not to contradict what I said about paying attention to who you spend time with. All I'm saying is that other people will have an influence on you so you must be mindful about that while simultaneously being genuine and personable.

Remember, we don't get in life what we want; we get in life, what we are. Who we associate with plays a huge role in who we become.

The Big Four Must-Have Relationships

In his book *Rich Dad Poor Dad*, Robert Kiyosaki points out that business and investing are team sports. He goes on to explain that the most successful are often those that work with a team of advisors and mentors rather than trying to get there by themselves. In his book, he illustrates the contrast between his rich dad and his biological poor dad. His rich dad was a man that started with nothing and grew a business empire all while surrounding himself with a team of other smart business people and advisors. His poor dad, however, was the highly educated government employee that "knew it all" and never wanted to pay for professional advice. He would rarely seek out help from advisors since he saw them as expensive or unnecessary and ultimately ended up poor and broke by the end of his life. Kiyosaki's book devotes a lot to the subject of financial literacy but more importantly, it also illustrates the importance of surrounding yourself with a good team and associating with people that will help you succeed.

Wait, am I saying that you need assistance from others to be successful? You bet I am! Just consider all high achievers, from CEO's to movie stars and professional athletes and any of those that go on to accomplish great things in life. They all have a habit of surrounding themselves with others that are smarter, stronger, wiser, and more experienced. They will seek out professional coaches and trainers to help them develop their skills and progress towards their goals. They will look for experts in their areas of interest and learn from mentors. They will find associations or interest groups so they can meet and work with others that are also on a similar journey.

GOOD RELATIONSHIPS BREED SUCCESS

That is completely opposite to how most people prefer to approach their goals and dreams. Most people would rather not share their ideas and dreams with others for fear of criticism. Most people would rather be the smartest, strongest or wealthiest person in the room and will usually avoid asking for advice out of fear that it makes them look weak or unsure about themselves. Most people want to show others that they are confident and wise and will rely on their own insights and experiences over seeking help from coaches and advisors. Most people aren't comfortable leveraging their network of connections to help accomplish their goals for fear they will be accused of using others. Most people end up going it alone. Most people achieve mediocre results. Is it any surprise most people never reach their life's goals or fulfill their highest potential?

Luckily, I trust that you are not like most people and are open to challenging your old limiting beliefs. Keep one thing in mind; no matter how good you are now or how successful you've been in the past, you will never outgrow your need for the advice and wisdom of others. I'm not saying that you can't make your own decisions or that you need to check with others before doing anything substantial. What I am saying is that is it wise to seek the counsel of others. I am saying that you should be leveraging your network and that you should always be building new relationships. It's no secret that the most successful among us got there with the support and guidance of others. It should be no different for you.

Even if the results you want depend entirely on you doing the work, there are still four significant relationships that you must establish and maintain to reach your fullest potential. These big four relationships are mentors, coaches, mastermind groups and mentees. In every field, from professional athletes to musicians to business leaders, you will find the most successful and effective among them have these four relationships in place at all times. Let's take a quick look at each one.

#1 - The Mentor

Having a great mentor or set of mentors in your life will gain you more benefits on your path to success than any other relationship you'll ever have. Regardless of your goal, just about everyone can benefit from having a mentor. All of the greats have had at least one mentor on their path to success. For example, Jim Rohn was a mentor to Tony Robbins; Steven Covey mentored Brian Tracy; Benjamin Graham became a mentor to Warren Buffett who in turn became a mentor to Bill Gates; Steve Jobs was a mentor to Mark Zuckerberg; and the greatest mentor of all, Master Yoda brought out the best in Luke Skywalker as he transformed him into a Jedi Knight. Okay, just making sure you were paying attention.

So what exactly is a mentor? A mentor is someone who has been down that path you are going or who has achieved the level of success you want and can share their wisdom, skills and knowledge with you. A mentor is someone that should inspire you and perhaps even intimidate you a little. The mentor/mentee relationship is always a one-to-one relationship and one where they get to know each other. Most often, a mentoring relationship is not a formal agreement but will form over time as trust and openness are established in the relationship.

Finding a mentor may not be as hard as you would imagine and most successful people enjoy helping the next generation succeed. While you shouldn't just go up to someone that has the level of success you want and bluntly ask them to be your mentor, because that is the quickest way to turn them away, you should always be on the look-out for those that have the potential to be your mentors and seek to build relationships with them. Most people are reluctant to commit their time and energy to such a responsibility, so just going around trying to create formal mentoring relationships is the least useful approach to take, especially when approaching complete strangers.

Rather, a mentor should be someone who notices you and takes an interest in what you are doing or what you've already accomplished. If you can't impress them enough with your current accomplishments or your enthusiasm and vision for your goals, then why should they spend time and energy mentoring you? Most mentors will do it because they genuinely want to help you, they enjoy seeing others succeed and they love to share their knowledge, insights and experiences with others. To create a mentor relationship, start by you reaching out to them and asking for advice or feedback. Over time, this will develop into more frequent contact and openness, which then matures into a true mentoring relationship. Often times, the mentors themselves may not even realize they are your mentors until long after the relationship has been in place. It has to feel natural and only then, can you really thank someone for being your mentor.

So what are the benefits of having a good mentor? There are many great benefits to having a mentor but here are few of the most important. A good mentor will be someone that can share knowledge and experiences with you that are unique to your goals and current situation. A mentor is often someone that has already had the success you are looking to achieve and can share first-hand knowledge of the industry. This will give you an enormous advantage and can cut your learning curve significantly. Additionally, mentors can give you access to their contacts, which often has taken them many years to establish. Having the recommendation of a successful mentor will open opportunities that may have otherwise never been available to you.

A mentor will be someone you can share ideas within a safe and confidential environment. Learning from a mentor will stretch your thinking as they offer you alternate perspectives and solutions. This is usually the most valuable benefit of a mentoring relationship, as it will significantly influence who you become. Sure, the access to contacts and industry knowledge are great, but the transformative and growth process that changes your thinking and actions are much more valuable in the long run. Remember, it's about teaching you to fish for yourself and not just giving you a fish to eat today. Finally, a good mentor will be some who points out areas you need to improve in and will often give you valuable feedback that you can use for personal growth.

#2 - The Coach

A coach is different from a mentor in the sense that they don't necessarily need to have personally achieved the level of success or skills you want to achieve. However, a good professional coach will be someone who has the training, tools, and techniques needed to get the most out of you. Take for example the legendary NBA coach Phil Jackson. While he played in the NBA and was a part of championship teams, he was not considered an exceptional basketball player. However, as a coach he had an incredible track record for leading teams and has racked up accomplishments such as having the highest winning percentage of any NBA coach, leading the Chicago Bulls to six championships and the Los Angeles Lakers to five. No doubt he was working with some of the greatest players ever such as Michael Jordan and Kobe Bryant, but Coach Jackson was effective at taking his star athletes and bringing out the best in them to create unstoppable teams.

It was his guidance, his discipline, his strategy and... well, his coaching that turned exceptional individual players into amazing basketball teams. Even though a coach never personally scores a single point for the team, a good coach can be the difference between an average team and one that wins championships. Imagine how a professional sports team would perform if they had no coach. How successful could they really be? It works the same way for your own personal goals. A coach is critical not just for professional athletes but also for entrepreneurs, business leaders, and sales professionals.

Hiring a coach is one of the best personal investments you'll ever make yet few people ever want to admit that they need a business or personal coach. When you tell someone you have a mentor, it sounds impressive and gives others the impression that you're making more of yourself. However, when you tell people that you have a life coach or a business coach, they look at you like you've just admitted to receiving counseling or that you've come to the end of your rope and need professional help. Nothing could be further from the truth and you should hire a coach before you feel like you need one.

Much like a personal trainer at the gym, a coach should be someone that can keep you accountable, asks you hard questions and keeps you progressing toward your goals. A good coach is will also help you develop specific skills and help you maximize your personal strengths and talents. They will provide an outside perspective and can point out deficiencies or blind-spots that we're often unwilling to acknowledge. A good coach will also give you positive reinforcement and encouragement to keep you motivated. Unlike a mentoring relationship, most coaches are professionals and the relationship is often a formal agreement and usually has some sort of compensation involved. Coaches, professional trainers, consultants and advisors all fall into this category.

Your mentor and coach can occasionally be the same person, but they usually are not. The reason for this is that your mentor is there as a strategic and inspirational role model while your coach plays more of a tactical and daily role in your success. Your coach should be working closely with you and meeting regularly to assess progress on your skill development or goals. A coach doesn't necessarily need to be pursuing the same goals as you nor do they need to have already achieved the same level of success that you want. Rather, they are specialized and trained to help you get to where you want to go. They have techniques and information that will help you develop and maximize your potential.

Ultimately, however, you are still the one that needs to do the work. Just as Phil Jackson transformed exceptional basketball players into incredible basketball teams, your coach will get you to work both harder and smarter as you aim for peak performance. Whether you are running a solo marathon, writing a book or building the next Google, you will need a coach of some kind. Either to help you develop a particular skill or to give you tactical advice and techniques to reach your goal. You put yourself at a disadvantage by not utilizing the benefits of a good coach.

#3 - The Mastermind Group

Aside from successful mentors and hard-core coaches, we also need to interact with peers that are on the same path as we are. We need others that we can relate with, someone to share stories from the trenches with and someone to help with accountability. The term mastermind was coined by Napoleon Hill when he formally introduced the concept in his book *Think and Grow Rich*. His larger volume, *The Laws of Success* goes into greater detail of what the mastermind is and how every member benefits from belonging to such a group. He defined the mastermind group principal as

"The coordination of knowledge and effort of two or more people, who work toward a definite purpose, in the spirit of harmony."

He went on to explain that

"No two minds ever come together without thereby creating a third, invisible, intangible force, which may be likened to a third mind [the master mind]."

While its definition has been around for almost a hundred years, it has only been in the recent past that the term mastermind group has been used more widely to describe the business or personal groups that are seeking a common interest. A simple business example of this when the board of a corporation and its members work with the CEO for the best interest of the company and its shareholders.

In essence, the members of a mastermind group come together to offer each other a combination of brainstorming, education, peer accountability and support in the group setting. As each of the individual business and personal skills are sharpened, the entire group benefits and simultaneously helps each member achieve even more individual success.

The 'magic' of a mastermind group is that when all of the members are working together in harmony, there is an incredible level of synergy that goes on to create a dynamic that only exists when the group comes together. This is more than just 'group think' or a vibe that is felt like those at motivational seminars and conferences. It's more than just emotions and herd mentality. Rather, this magic creates a sort of group mind (i.e. The Mastermind) through which the individual members can access creativity, ideas and knowledge that would not have been available to them otherwise. It may hard to believe, but until you've been in such a setting, it's hard to comprehend the flows of energy and thoughts that takes place within a mastermind group. Mastermind groups sizes can range from just two people to over one hundred members but even Napoleon Hill stated the optimal group size was 6-7 members.

A mastermind group is NOT a class or workshop. While you can occasionally bring in educational speakers, this is not the core purpose. A mastermind group is NOT about group coaching or mentoring. The facilitator or founder of the group should not be the only one teaching and advising all of the others. Everyone in the group contributes and everyone receives. A mastermind group is NOT a networking group. While new connections are indeed made and you'll occasionally get new leads and learn of new opportunities, this is not the purpose of the group. A mastermind group requires commitment and confidentiality of all the members. There should be support, honesty and respect between the members.

As it relates to SHARK Belief, the reason we all need a Mastermind Group is so that we can have others to meet with regularly solely for the purpose of discussing our goals and challenges with each other. If you are an entrepreneur, then your mastermind group should also include other entrepreneurs also on a similar path. If you want to learn to program, then you should meet with other programmers. If you are training for a triathlon, then your group should also include others that are training for one as well.

Finding others that you can relate with as it pertains to your goals will not only keep you accountable, it will also have an enormous impact on your motivation and excitement. This is especially critical during those inevitable times of trials and frustrations that will cause us to question our pursuit and tempt us to quit. It is during our times of failure that we most want to retreat into our caves and avoid others but this is precisely the time when we need to remain close to others. It is during these times that the mastermind group produces some of its greatest benefits.

Seeking out those that are already doing what you want to do is one of the most effective and quickest ways to jumpstart progress toward your goals. When I decided to write my first book, I had no idea how to publish a book or where to get started. One of the first things I did was connect with a Book Publishers and Marketing MeetUp group in my area. By meeting other published and aspiring authors, I was able to cut my learning curve and was also inspired to see their published books. Whenever I had a question, this was the best group of people to ask for advice. It was also comforting to know that I wasn't the only one feeling confused and overwhelmed. Many others were on the same journey as I and it was great to have someone to share ideas with. I took the same approach when first learning about computer programming, web and mobile app development, stock investing and entrepreneurship. Frequent contact with others pursuing similar goals was invaluable. It was also a major contributor to me ultimately achieving my aim. Whether developing a new skill, learning a new language or building a new business, you should employ the use of a mastermind group and accountability partners to help you get there.

#4 - The Mentee

You have now seen the importance of having mentors, coaches, and accountability partners. These relationships are often the catalysts that take us to the next level in our personal development and ultimately help us reach our successes. Another key relationship you should always maintain is having your own mentee. You should always make time to mentor or coach someone else. Perhaps you feel that you still have a long way to go and that you couldn't possibly offer someone else advice. I say start with what you do know and go from there. Be a sounding board for their ideas. Teach them what you've learned so far and share the progress you've made toward you own goals. Teach them what you've learned about SHARK Belief, recommend blogs that have helped you or simply share an inspirational quote with them.

There is always someone that you can help and you will find few things more satisfying in life than helping someone else reach their potential. It is extremely gratifying to help change the life of someone else and see him or her succeed. You'll also notice that you will work just a little bit harder when you know that someone else sees you as their role model. Realizing you'll be explaining concepts that you only recently learned will force you to get a better grasp on them. You'll find that you learn faster when you know you have to teach it to someone else. In your pursuit of success, remember to leave a trail for those coming behind you. When someone needs help getting to the next level, look back and offer them a helping hand. There is a law of reciprocity in our universe and paradoxically, it is those that give the most that often receive the most.

"Talent wins games, but teamwork and intelligence wins championships."

- Michael Jordan

How to Become a People Person

By now you should understand the importance of your connections and those you associate with. Perhaps you're also becoming a little uneasy at the thought of having to engage in that dreaded activity we call "networking." However, even if you don't plan on becoming a social butterfly, there is no doubt that interpersonal skills are some of the most profitable skills you can develop.

For over ten years, I worked in an environment that was predominantly engineers. We had everything from mechanical and electrical engineers to software and industrial engineers. It didn't take long for me to notice a predominant trend in the engineers that rose to the top ranks. It was the engineers that had the best communication and leadership skills that were promoted and paid the most. Sure, they also had excellent technical skills and had proven that with their results but they were not usually considered the best or smartest engineers in their departments. Rather, the unique characteristics that put them amongst the most valuable people on the team were their ability to work with others and to communicate effectively. The engineers that were noticed were those that could lead technical teams while also being able to communicate with the business leaders. It was those engineers that could create and cultivate new relationships with a broad range of people. Essentially, it came down to having good people skills. Having strong technical knowledge was the minimum requirement to work there anyway so the key differentiator was interpersonal ability.

In every industry, it has proven that the most profitable skills to have, after you have the basics required for that particular field, are good people skills. Yes, there are always exceptions and there are certainly some narrow areas in which you could get away with being a complete jerk and still have people tolerate it (for a while anyway) due to your extraordinary skills. Some sports stars for example. But even in these cases, the star or genius will eventually burn enough bridges that even their extraordinary skill will be passed over because leaders do not enjoy having toxic people on their teams.

Do you need to work on becoming a better people person? Absolutely! Even if you don't plan on being a highly connected power broker and would rather maintain a small, tight-knit social circle, you are still going to need some critical interpersonal skills for building and maintaining significant relationships. Two of my favorite books in this category are Dale Carnegie's *How To Win Friends And Influence People* and Keith Ferrazzi's *Never Eat Alone*.

I highly recommend you read both of them but here are ten easy tips to help you with you with your social skills.

1. Smile – Sounds simple but most people don't do it often enough. It's especially important to smile when you first meet someone or if you want to make yourself approachable. I'm not talking about keeping that cheesy plastic smile plastered on your face all evening (you'll look like you're on drugs!) but rather, to produce that occasional natural smile of yours when meeting or talking with others. Smiling will make you more attractive to others and you'll also seem more trustworthy and approachable. Smiling is contagious and others will usually smile back at you so give it a shot. Surprisingly, smiling also has some significant health benefits. It releases endorphins, lowers stress and anxiety and ultimately helps your body's immune system. Smile more often.

2. Remember their name. A person's name (or whatever they like to be called) is the sweetest sound to them and also their favorite word. I'm always impressed when someone remembers my name, especially when I barely know them or when I can't remember their name. The mere fact that they

took time and effort to learn my name makes me want to learn theirs even more. It shows respect and awareness for others when you take the time to remember and use their name which in turn will make you more respected and memorable.

3. Listen – It's simple and we've all heard it before, but when someone else is talking, just listen. Resist the urge to cut them off and jump in with your comments. Actively listening to what they are saying and paying attention to the conversation will make you an excellent conversationalist even if you don't say much! People can notice when you're just waiting for them to stop talking so that you can begin talking about something entirely unrelated. People can also notice when you're not paying attention to them and looking around the room for a better person to talk to.

4. Compliment and praise others – Make it a habit of pointing out and saying good things about other people. Recognize other's strengths or attractive attributes and point them out. If someone has a new car, compliment them on it. If you notice some has a new haircut, point it out and make them feel special. However, people don't appreciate flattery and false praise, so make sure you're genuine and sincere when complimenting others.

5. Focus on the other person. Speak about what they are interested in. Ask questions and show a genuine interest in others. The majority of people like to talk about themselves and their interests more than anything else. If you give them this opportunity, they will enjoy talking with and being around you. They easiest ways to do this is by asking them questions.

6. Gratitude – Show sincere appreciation for others. This is especially important as a leader or influencer. I'm always amazed by how powerful a simple thank you note or phone call can be. If you're mindful of others and show a genuine appreciation, you will be amazed at how much others will be willing to do for you. Also, wouldn't you rather be around someone that shows sincere gratitude for the things in their life over someone that is constantly complaining?

7. Be Agreeable – You know those people that like to argue with everyone and contradict ideas or point out flaws? They always have to be right and make it a point to prove others wrong. Don't be that person! When having a conversation, it's okay to be agreeable and let others have their way from time to time. Sometimes, you just have to go with the flow.

8. Try to see things from their point of view. Let's face it, not everyone is going to agree with your or share your opinion. During times of difference, do your best to see things from their point of view before jumping to conclusions. You may gain a new perspective or insight as to why some people see things a certain way which will make you an even better people person.

9. Allow others to save face after mistakes or failure and always admit when you're wrong. Never criticize someone in public or in front others. There will be times when you're offended or when people fail and let you down. Let others save face and dignity by keeping your critique or dissatisfaction a private matter between you two. Berating someone in front of their friends or coworkers will almost always gain you a permanent

adversary. People find it hard to forgive when they've been publicly humiliated.

10. Just as others will make mistakes from time to time, you also will offend or let others down. Do your best not to, but when you do, quickly admit that you're wrong and apologize to the other person. People want good relationships with others and admitting when you're wrong often relieves the other person just as much as it does you. This will also gain you a tremendous amount of respect from others since it's our leaders and the emotionally mature that can admit when they are wrong.

11. Use Humor – Don't be so serious all the time. People like to laugh and have fun, so learn when to crack a joke or even make fun of yourself. It shouldn't be excessive but it will certainly make you more enjoyable to be around if you remember to keep things light from time to time.

Added Bonus! - I shouldn't have to say this but unfortunately, it is a huge reason some people struggle when interacting with others so it must be said. Be mindful of your own personal hygiene and appearance. Simple things like body odor or bad breath can be a huge turn-off and a distraction to others. Also, please don't overdo the cologne/perfume! You may not notice it but they certainly will. Strong smells, good or bad, may create a barrier when trying to connect with other people. Beyond just smells and appearance, make yourself easy to be around. I'm not saying to not be yourself, but simple things like showing good manners, wearing clean and presentable clothes and personal etiquette play a huge role in likability. It's all about being self-aware and mindful of how others perceive you. I promise, you'll thank me later.

The list above is certainly not a comprehensive one and there are countless books, articles and courses on subjects of interpersonal relationships, networking, and effective communication, which can help you become a better people person. The list above, however, is a great starting point and contains some keys to everyday interactions and good relationships. While these tips will help you improve your interpersonal skills, it's also important to remember that not everyone is going to like you or want to work with you. You certainly won't like everyone either, nor should you. That's okay. It's a part of life and no big deal.

Some people can get so caught up in wanting to be liked by everyone that they begin to lose focus on what's truly important. Remember that you're dealing other human beings and they'll probably have bad days too. Don't be so quick to judge if someone blows you off or is rude or doesn't take an interest in you right away. Consider that they might be having a bad day, perhaps they're working to a tight deadline or maybe they are reacting to something else in their lives and their actions are entirely unrelated to you. Everyone has both good and bad qualities about them and you'll need to learn how to work with less-than-perfect people. You don't necessarily need to develop an intimate friendship with everyone but you shouldn't be disrespectful either. I have done business with many people I didn't particularly like, but we respected each other and were able to accomplish things together. Sometimes people come around and they learn to like you or vice versa, and other times, you just move on.

Relationships are a critical component to reaching your goals and a key element of the SHARK Belief Success Code. The people we associate with will influence our beliefs, our knowledge, and our habits. Our relationships will most certainly impact our thinking and this is important because all of the SHARK Belief elements begin inside the mind. We ultimately become like those we associate with so it's important to be mindful of this fact and choose wisely. Make an effort to align yourself with those pursuing similar goals and to connect with those that have already achieved what you're after. I'll say it again, you don't get in life what you want, you get in life what you are. Those you choose to associate with regularly will have an enormous impact on who you become. Remember, SHARK Belief is all about change and becoming the person that achieves the success you're aiming for.

CHAPTER SEVEN

Knowledge Is Power

"It is important to view knowledge as sort of a semantic tree; make sure you understand the fundamental principles, i.e. the trunk and big branches before you get into the leaves (details) or there is nothing for them to hang on to."

- Elon Musk

When it comes to gaining knowledge in a wide variety of topics, one of my role models has always been the billionaire entrepreneur and technologist Elon Musk. At age 10, he discovered computing and taught himself programming which ultimately lead to him creating and selling his first video game by age 12. After college, Elon went on to found an internet company which was sold for $340 million while he was still in his twenties. He then co-founded an online financial services company, which was later named PayPal and was eventually bought by eBay for $1.5 billion dollars.

Still only 30 years old and already a successful serial entrepreneur, Elon Musk decided it was time to move away from Silicon Valley and pursue his childhood dreams of space exploration. He began by learning from experts in the space industry and sought to understand its challenges and opportunities. One thing Elon Musk does extremely well is concentrating on a topic that interests him and immersing himself in the subject to learn everything and anything he can about it. He did this with the space industry and was soon found studying old manuals on Soviet-era rockets, reading books on aeronautics and researching the potential of human travel to Mars.

Within a short period, Elon Musk was one of the most informed people in the space industry and had built up a personal network of some of the world's foremost experts on rockets, satellites and space travel. In 2002, he founded SpaceX and is now launching rockets and transporting cargo to the International Space Station for NASA. The company also has its sights set on the colonization of Mars. In addition to SpaceX, Elon Musk has gone on to co-found the electric car company Tesla Motors and is also the Chairman of Solar City, the renewable energy company that he also conceptualized and funded. He has shown an incredible ability to both learn about and execute successfully in a broad range of industries. This characteristic is a perfect example of an essential element in SHARK Belief; Knowledge. Elon Musk will determine what his aim is and then goes on gaining the necessary knowledge and understanding needed to accomplish his goals. His knowledge is acquired through various means such as his personal research as well as through strategic relationships and learning from experts.

Elon Musk clearly understands that gaining specific knowledge is paramount to successfully reaching his goals and he never lets the lack of knowledge stop him from getting started. He seeks out what needs to learn, gains understanding and then begins to formulate solutions and ideas from his newfound knowledge. He is not afraid to risk failure and often learns the most from his mistakes. He puts his knowledge to work by taking action and gains tremendous insight that helps him succeed. Elon Musk is a life-long learner and continues to expand his already vast understanding of highly complex topics. Luckily, you and I don't need to have the genius-level knowledge that Elon Musk has to begin pursuing our goals, but there is no doubt that success in any field will require that we have some fundamental knowledge about our own specific objectives.

What is Knowledge?

This sounds like a simple question but do you really know what knowledge is? We've all heard sayings like "knowledge is power" or "an investment in knowledge pays the best interest." I hope you agree that knowledge is important and something you must acquire along your journey to success. One thing to realize is that *information* is not knowledge! We are currently living in a time where a vast amount of information is being created each day and we have more information easily available to us than at any other time in history. However, while information does play a significant role, having more of it does not necessarily mean we have become more knowledgeable. In short, knowledge is having an understanding or familiarity with a particular subject. Knowledge is something that we *acquire* through the processes of learning and experience and is done by synthesizing facts and information for our use.

The K in SHARK Belief represents Knowledge. Knowledge is somewhat philosophical in its definition and has been debated for thousands of years. Scientists, philosophers, and religious teachers have all given different opinions on what knowledge truly is. There are different types of knowledge, but in relation to using knowledge for attaining success, I will primarily be referring to *explicit* knowledge and *procedural* knowledge. Explicit knowledge is that which can be easily transmitted to others and readily accessed or verbalized while procedural knowledge refers to having an internal understanding of how to do something or how something works.

Knowledge is essential to achieving your goals because success in your chosen area will require that you have information and understanding that is specific to your goal. It would be tough to successfully start a technology-based business if you knew absolutely nothing about the workings of the Internet, software or electronics. You wouldn't necessarily be required to write code or solder a circuit board yourself, but you would be at a serious disadvantage if you knew nothing about the latest technology or processes required to be successful in that field. Even a simple goal such as losing ten pounds in five months would require that you gain some basic knowledge of diet and exercise. If you want to be successful in reaching your goal, it is dangerous to assume that you already possess all of the knowledge you need about your particular pursuit. Even if you've attempted that specific goal in the past, it's always best to reassess your knowledge on the topic and seek to gain more understanding. What you don't know may be holding you back from achieving the level of success you desire.

Knowledge is (*Potential*) Power!

As critical as knowledge is to you being able to successfully achieve your goal, please remember that it is just one of six elements in SHARK Belief. It is not the end-all be-all and the reality is that knowledge is only *potential* power. Until you take action on the knowledge you've acquired, you are nothing more than latent potential. It can be exciting to learn new things, attend seminars and continue to accumulate more knowledge. But until you execute on it, all that information will do you no good. I know some brilliant people that are highly knowledgeable in a wide variety of topics. They are like walking encyclopedias, yet they continue to fail and never seem to make any real progress in life. I struggled to understand why my very smart and "talented" friends were never successful. Then I realized that it takes a lot more than just having knowledge. These guys had a lot of general knowledge and some were almost experts in certain areas. However, they lacked focused action towards accomplishing a goal and they rarely used the other SHARK Belief elements which are critical to success. Things such as Habits, Skills and Beliefs. I'm a huge proponent of education and I have no doubt that knowledge is critical to success. However, if that were all that was required, then our University Professors and Teachers would be the richest and most successful people in the world.

A common trap that people tend to fall into is what is called *Paralysis by Analysis*. This is the state of over-analyzing (or over-thinking) a situation to the point that a decision is never made or action is never taken, in effect paralyzing the outcome. Have you ever wanted to pursue a goal but could never seem to get started because you felt that you needed more information about it the topic first? "Just one more book or one more seminar and then I'll be ready!" It never ends. In fact, after a certain point, more information will just confuse you because you reach a point where you start seeing contradicting ideas about what works best. Every guru will have their own "best way" to do something.

There is an infinite amount of information out there and you can find thousands of books and articles on just about any topic. Research any topic and you will find arguments both for and against it. I assure you, you will never know it all and you don't need to know it all before getting started on working towards your goal! At some point, you have to decide that you've learned enough about the basics to get started and begin taking action. It is after you take the first step that the real learning begins. Take entrepreneurship for example. You'll never learn how to be an entrepreneur just from reading books. If you want to learn how to create new products, lead teams, or build a startup, then you have to get out there and do it. Chances are, you already know the basics but that doesn't excuse from continued learning. In fact, you'll gain a tremendous amount of knowledge just by taking action and doing something.

Working towards your goal, even before you "know enough" is the best way to cut the learning curve. You don't need to memorize everything you read or be able to teach it to others before you get started. You must be willing to make some mistakes along the way. The learning will never stop, but you must learn and gain more understanding *while* in pursuit of your goal. You'll never really "know" how to do something until you begin taking action. As they say, experience is the best teacher. Sometime you win, and other times you learn. This is especially true for gaining the procedural type of knowledge. We all have different ways of learning, but hands-on experience has proven to be the most effective for most people.

Success Does Not Require a Genius

It's easy to think that unless you're a genius, you'll never be successful. This notion comes from hearing stories of successful prodigies such as Bill Gates and Mark Zuckerberg. It's easy to feel intimated when you ready about legendary geniuses such as Albert Einstein and Nikola Tesla. But what you should remember is that there are also countless millions of other highly successful individuals that you will never read about in headline news. Most of these people have ordinary IQ's, but they are using the techniques taught in SHARK Belief to achieve extraordinary success.

One of the most famous businessmen in recent times is the billionaire entrepreneur and philanthropist Sir Richard Branson. He is the founder of the business conglomerate Virgin Group, which comprises of more than 400 companies. He is most famous for his Virgin Records, Virgin Airlines, and Virgin Galactic enterprises but is involved in just about every industry. What many people don't know is that Richard Branson had poor academic performance as a student. Branson himself said, "At school, I was dyslexic and a dunce." This did not stop his ambitions and upon finishing school, he learned everything he could about the music industry and eventually launched his own successful record label.

Through the decades, Branson has continued to expand his knowledge and has grown his business empire to the point it now reaches just about every industry. He has since launched an airline company, a telephone company, a Vodka brand, authored several books, created several media companies and is even working on a space tourism company, just to name a few. He has acquired a great deal of knowledge in a lot of different areas. Not bad for a dunce! Branson has shown us that you don't have to be born a genius to become highly knowledgeable and that success does not require that you first be an academic prodigy. More often than not, it's not about talent but it's about effort.

Having specific knowledge is critical to achieving your goals because success in your chosen area will require that you have particular information and understanding about what you're aiming to achieve. Everyone has different ways they prefer to learn but here are some of the key sources of knowledge you should consider.

Reading – Books, journals, blogs, Wikipedia and anything written about your goal and the information about it. Most industries, hobbies, sports or groups will all have their own vocabulary and particular language. Just understanding the related terminology is half the battle and the best way to overcome this is by repeated exposure. Just start reading about the topic or goal you want to achieve. Even if you don't understand it all, you'll begin to see patterns as certain words and ideas will start to show up frequently. Reading is the oldest and easiest way to gain information and understanding about something you don't know. Living in the information age offers you access to anything at the tips of your finger. There is no excuse for not being able to get information on something you want to learn. You just have to be willing to put in the time and effort to seek it out.

Audio and Video – Not everyone considers themselves to be a "reader" or wants to sit down for hours to make time for it. I get it. Luckily, for those of us that are more visually or audibly inclined, we have tremendous resources to make this easier. You can find a video online for just about anything you want through sites like YouTube or Vimeo. There are many "schools" online that specialize in just about everything and many of these are free. We have access to hundreds of thousands of free podcasts and I guarantee you, there is a podcast about the topic you're interested in. I love listening to audio books while driving or doing some mundane task around the house. You can even increase the speed of the video or audio you consume so you can learn at 2X or 3X speed!

Other People – Don't know what to read or which videos to watch? Then the absolute best way to start is by reaching out to others that have accomplished what you want to achieve and finding out how they did it. Ask them what information they believe you should learn, what groups are they a part of, what websites do they visit, what books do the read and so on. What's their story? There is no better way to change your beliefs and improve your knowledge about your goal than by talking with others who have done it before you. Their wisdom from experience and years of learning will do wonders for shortening your learning curve. If you live in a major city, you can find other like-minded people in your locale through platforms such as MeetUp, Facebook Groups & LinkedIn. You can even reach out to others in different parts of the world through online forums and groups. The resources are endless and gaining knowledge from others has never been easier in our now highly-connected world. You've read just how critical relationships are to your success. Gaining knowledge is one the reasons why.

Experience – The best way to learn is by doing. Nothing beats hands-on personal experience. Eventually, the time will come when you've read all you can, have seen enough videos, listened to enough audio and received all the advice you can handle. You will have to take action at some point and I guarantee you that time will come before you "feel ready." The ultimate teacher is experience. Until you begin to work towards your goal by taking personal action, you will not internalize the learning and knowledge through just reading and listening. It's wise to be prepared by learning what you can before you take action but true wisdom and understanding come from real-life experiences. Most of the time, it's uncomfortable, scary, and maybe a little painful but growth will require that you move beyond your current comfort zone. You will learn from your mistakes as well as from your successes.

Learning Hacks

In the science fiction movie the Matrix, there is a scene where Neo is training and fighting Morpheus. The entire scene takes place inside their minds and is a simulation of the Matrix world. As they enter the virtual dojo, Neo has just been "trained" in the various forms of martial arts and is now an expert fighter. How did he learn to do this? Much like updating a computer software program, various "programs" were uploaded into Neo's brain and he instantly had knowledge in all sorts of fighting techniques. Later in the movie, they continue to upload anything they want to "learn" into their minds. Fighting, shooting and even pilot skills. I believe the day will come where the man-machine interface will allow us to learn new information almost instantaneously. Until that day, we'll have to go about it just like any other normal person and make time to learn the things we want to know.

I like to tell everyone that the most important thing I learned in college was learning how to learn. I was a terrible student in high school and it's a miracle I graduated on time. Upon my arrival in college, I quickly realized that if I were going to survive academically, then it was critical that I quickly overcame some bad learning habits and deficiencies. My poor performance in high school was not because I was dumb, or a slow learner or because I was ADHD. I am none of those but rather I lacked some essential learning skills and techniques that would have helped me perform better in class. While at University, I was able to pick up some useful tips and tricks that I continue to use today.

Learning how to learn is a key ability that you should seek to master and improve throughout your life. If you can learn to teach yourself anything, there is no limit to where you can go. Just like any other skill, your ability to learn can be developed and improved drastically. Quit telling yourself things like "I've never been a reader," "I have a bad memory" or "That's really hard, I'm not smart enough to learn something that complex." Most people are unaware of the incredible potential of their own brain. Your mind works much like a muscle and with proper training and exercise, it will become stronger regardless of your age or past mental performances.

Here are some key learning tips I picked up along the way:

Ask Questions – Sounds like common sense but many people are afraid to ask questions because they don't want to look foolish or feel insecure around "smarter people." I have found that some of the most intelligent people I know are actually the ones that ask the most questions! That is because asking questions is a core aspect to active learning. Even if you're learning on your own or reading a book, asking yourself some questions along the way will help you to process the information more effectively. These questions will keep your mind engaged while learning something new and will make it more likely that you'll retain the information. Some examples are: "What is the main idea here?", "How does this fit in with other information I've learned?" and "What information don't I understand and look into later?"

Take it step further and write down the answers to those questions as you're learning. If it's a central idea, then write it out. If it's something you don't understand, then write that out as a reminder to look into it later. Even if you don't review your notes later, just the simple act of questioning and writing these thoughts will keep you engaged while learning something new. It's not about how much time you spend learning but rather about how effectively that time is used. Active learning, even while reading or watching a video will ensure that you maximize this time to gain new knowledge.

Take Notes – Whether it's physically writing them out or in doing it electronically on your phone or computer, taking notes is essential to gaining new knowledge. You will not remember everything you read or hear on the first pass and unless you take notes, it will be forgotten within a few days. The act of taking notes helps to reinforce critical information and will make it easier to remember later. There are many techniques around effective note taking so just find one that works best for you and give it a shot. I have found the simpler and easier, the better. You don't need to turn it into a science project and no one else is going to critique your notes. Just jot down your thoughts and ideas as you learn and you'll find your knowledge expanding quickly.

Reading Faster – We all want to read more but the problem is that we don't want to make time for the countless hours it will take to read all the books on our list. This is where speed-reading comes in handy. One of the first books I picked up while in college was a book called *How to Read a Book* by Mortimer Adler & Charles Van Doren. Eventually, I realized just how popular and useful this book was but when I first came across it at the library, I had never heard of it but somehow knew it would be a good place to start. I felt out of place and a little intimidated when I first arrived so admitting that I needed help with a basic skill like reading was a big deal to me in the college environment.

I was quite embarrassed as I walked up to the checkout counter and handed the book over to the librarian (this was pre-

Amazon!). He gave me a puzzled look and let out a small laugh as if to say, "doesn't everyone know how to read a book?" I didn't laugh. The truth is while most everyone is literate, understanding how to read a book effectively is a different skill entirely and one that can be learned over time. I was dead serious about improving my reading ability since I knew it would be key to not only surviving but for thriving over the next few years as I completed a highly technical degree program. I would be doing a lot of reading over the coming years.

Everyone will be required to read more information. Even if you don't plan on reading more books, learning some basic speed reading techniques will help you since you will likely be required to read increasing amounts of information online, at work and on your mobile devices. One simple technique that can increase your reading speed is to use a pencil or your finger to help guide your eyes across the words. Doing so will help you to keep focus by preventing you from going back and reading the same words repeatedly. People will often re-read what they just read and it's because they want to really grasp what they just read or because they are not focused on the material. Ironically, by using a guide to force yourself to move along the page, you will actually focus more and have a better comprehension of what you're reading without having to go back and read it again. There are also several good apps that can help you build your speed-reading ability.

Hardware Upgrade – Optimize Your Brain Power

The field of neuroscience has made vast advancements in recent years as we seek to better understand the complexities of the human mind. It is a fascinating field and recent discoveries now give us the power to "hack" into the brain to accelerate learning, improve focus and even control our thoughts. Most of these techniques do not require drugs or high-tech equipment. This is accessible to most people and just requires a little understanding of the methods. Your brain is like a supercomputer with your physical brain and bodily functions acting as the hardware equivalent and your thoughts and subconscious mind representing the software side. This brain/mind pair works together to act as the most powerful machine to ever exist. You can use this to your advantage and there are many things you can do to improve and optimize your brainpower. You can even "reprogram the mind" and change your thought patterns. More on that in the Beliefs chapter.

We're not yet at the point where we can double our IQ, but there are various techniques we can use to ensure that the brain is firing on all cylinders which will improve learning ability, enhance mental clarity and strengthen long-term memory.

Immerse Yourself

The best way to learn anything is to immerse yourself in the subject for a period of time just to absorb the main ideas and principals around the topic. There is information on every topic and industry readily available today and with enough time and effort, I truly believe you can learn anything. As I said, one of the best skills anyone can learn is to be able to learn quicker and more effectively. Rarely does this have anything to do with your IQ or being considered "smart." Instead, learning ability is more like any other skill that needs to be developed with practice and effective techniques. Here are seven essential techniques to accelerate your learning while you work on improving your ability to learn faster.

1. Learning during peak states – Do your best to control both your environment and your mental state before learning. Put yourself in an optimal state to accelerate your learning. Stay well hydrated and have some energy. A light snack, coffee or tea often helps me stay alert and focused while learning. Focus! Cut out the distractions for a short while. Turn off the phone and email alerts for 30 minutes at a time and you'll be amazed at how much more focused you can stay. Find a good place to learn. Learn during your peak mental energy states. Our bodies go through cycles during the day and there are specific windows of time where we have more energy and mental focus and that makes the best times to learn. I have found that I'm optimal after waking up and during early evening hours of the day. I have learned effectively during any time of the day but when I really need to focus and maximize my time and effort, I'll pick those two time windows.

2. Jot down notes or ideas while learning something new. It doesn't have to be a word for word duplication. Rather, it should just be some key points or words you picked up. This has never been easier with apps like Evernote and voice recorders.

3. Review before bed – When learning a tremendous amount of new information, review what you learned that day within an hour of going to sleep. Whether that's reading a summary, reviewing your notes, or discussing it with someone, find a way to refresh your memory of the key ideas learned. Doing so will activate these memory centers in the brain and will help solidify the new information and ideas while you sleep. You'll

find that doing this helps you to remember easier and increase your learning speed.

4. Share your knowledge with others. Trying to explain what you've just learned to someone will test you on fundamental concepts and will improve your memory recall. Additionally, it will force you to organize the information and may also reveal gaps in the learning. You don't have to be an expert to do this step, just explain what you've learned so far, even if that is just a few key words that you still don't understand. Talking through it and trying to explain it is one of the best ways to quickly learn a new topic. Test yourself now: Do you remember all six of the elements in **SHARK** Belief Success Code?

5. Be Curious – when learning anything new, the best thing you can do is ask questions. Don't just sit back and passively let the information flow your way. Instead, lay out some questions ahead of time about the topic and then go out and look for the answers. When you hear a new concept or word, ask yourself what it means, how it fits together with other things you just learned, or why it matters. You'll find that some of the most intelligent and skilled people are those that are always asking questions as they seek to understand. Doing so will help connect the dots and solidify new ideas.

6. Mix up the learning environment – There is no single "best way" to learn anything. We all learn differently and have preferred methods. Mixing up the environment and methods will help you accelerate your learning. Don't just sit back and read new material at your desk. Find audio you can listen to while driving or in the shower. Watch a video with someone

else and then discuss what you've just learned. Learn outside, learn at the coffee shop, learn with others, sit in a lecture, try hands-on training, and attend a workshop or class. Learn with some background music playing and learn in complete silence. Try mornings, evenings, alone and with groups. There are many ways to learn and trying a little of each will shorten your learning curve since each method of learning activates various areas of the brain. Combining this with some of the other tips mentioned will ensure you'll be learning at an accelerated rate.

7. Take breaks and get some sleep – Your brain can only handle so much inflow at a time before the learning process begins to slow. You can only focus for so long and you need to give you mind time to rest so the new information can "settle in". Remember, even after actively learning (reading, watching, or doing) your mind will continue to work subconsciously to help solidify the new material. Take regular short breaks throughout the learning process. Ensure that you're getting adequate sleep each night. The right amount of sleep varies for everyone, but this is one of the best things you can do for your brain apart from proper nutrition. When you sleep, your body works to cleanse your mind of certain chemicals and toxins that build up while you're awake. It helps to reset the brain so that when you wake up, you're ready for another round of learning and activity. Many of the great inventors and artists would often take naps while trying to solve a problem or think of new ideas. Mediation or a short nap will do wonders for the brain and will give you a renewed sense of

focus and clarity. It may sound counterintuitive, but taking a break or a nap will actually help you learn faster.

Mega Memory

There is a little-known competition hosted in the USA every year that is a "thinking game" tournament designed for mental athletes with incredible memories known as Memory Championships. It is a competition that requires the participants to quickly memorize things such as 117 random names and faces, shuffled decks of cards, the words in a book and long strings of numbers. The participants include people from all over the world and their ages range from those in their teens to grandparents. At first glance, you would think these people are all geniuses because they can perform incredible feats such as memorizing the exact order of multiple decks of shuffled cards after only studying them for a few minutes. However, what you'll find is that they do not have photographic memories and are generally no smarter than the average person. Instead, they have developed some simple memory techniques that anyone can learn to make their memory stronger. What these memory champions understand is that we aren't born with great memories but rather, great memories are made.

Much like strengthening your muscles with resistance training, you can improve your memory by testing it more often. The following are a few examples of simple techniques that anyone can use to help them remember anything. You could read entire books on the topic so I won't go into too much detail here but just be aware of them and research some additional techniques that may work for you.

Mental Snapshots – Creating a vivid and memorable mental images that are associated with the information you want to remember helps store it into long-term memory. It also makes it easier to remember because you recall the mental snapshot which acts as a "hook" to the information. These images can be real or imagined. In fact, the more ridiculous or exaggerated the image, the easier it will be to recall it. This helps when trying to remember boring things like facts and numbers.

Mnemonics – Many forms of mnemonics can help learners recall large pieces of information. Mnemonics are tools or learning techniques that help translate information into a form that makes it easier for the brain to remember. These come in the forms of musical jingles, names, phrases, and images. For example, the phrase "Please Excuse My Dear Aunt Sally" is commonly taught in schools as a way to remember the order of operations in math:

Parentheses, Exponents, Multiply, Divide, Add, and Subtract.

Memory Palace – A form of mnemonic, the so-called memory palace or mind palace is a technique that uses spatial visualization to help organize and recall information and is very popular with memory contest champions. It has been used for thousands of years and was popular among the Ancient Greeks and Romans.

Brain Health - If it's good for the body, it's good for the brain

There are three aspects to your health that deserve extra attention to optimize your brain function; your diet, your exercise, and your sleep.

Superfoods – Your brain weighs only two to three pounds, yet it consumes 20-30% of your body's total calories each day. What you eat will have a direct impact on your brain so it's important we give it the best fuel. Along with exercise, certain foods have shown to help with various aspects of our brain function including improved memory, focus, and mental clarity. Likewise, many foods and diets have adverse effects our brain power and will make it difficult to learn effectively and increase knowledge. Most of us have experienced that sluggish feeling after eating way too much sugar, carbs or junk food. It's hard enough just to stay awake let alone focus on learning something new. A chronically bad diet will have you feeling like this all of the time!

If you want to reach the next level of your success, you will need greater amounts of mental energy and focus. Some small changes to your diet will go a long way towards optimizing your mental power. I won't go into the long list of foods and drinks that are bad for your brain, but remember that in addition to eating better foods, you should also look to see what should be eliminated from your diet. If the food you're eating is not good for your body long-term, then it's even worse for your brain and its ability to function at peak state. The same can be said for things that damage the body and brain such as smoking, drug use, drinking alcohol and chemicals known to cause brain damage.

Give your brain optimal fuel to run on and it will work wonders for you. In general, the brain needs a balanced diet of proteins, healthy fats, vegetables and some carbohydrates. A lot of people say your brain needs grains and sugar since it runs on glucose but research has shown these things can actually leave you feeling foggy and hinder brain function. Instead, your brain likes healthy fats as well as nutrition from vegetables. Here is a short list of superfoods known to optimize brain function: Water, green tea, coffee, dark chocolate, avocados, blueberries, walnuts, almonds, salmon and other fatty fish, coconut oil, olive oil and dark green leafy vegetables. Minimize processed foods, preservatives, and artificial flavorings or colors. Maximize fresh whole foods, raw foods and those closer to their natural state. I also highly suggest taking multivitamins (and other supplements) to ensure you're getting all the vitamins and minerals your body needs.

Exercise – I'm not saying you have to start a serious bodybuilding routine or lose 30 pounds to reap the benefits of a better brain. However, some regular physical activity will certainly provide a boost to mental capacities, helping you learn more effectively. Research has shown that even just a small amount of regular physical exercise has significant benefits to your brainpower. Fifteen minutes of jogging or some light aerobic exercise is enough to improve the blood flow and the oxygen levels going to the brain. Regular exercise also reduces stress, regulates your hormones and releases endorphins. I've had some of my best ideas while jogging or just after exercising. As noted in the Habit chapter, many of the successful have established a habit regular exercise or some form of physical activity. Beyond the benefits to your physique and bodily health, exercise has long been proven to be one of the best ways to boost brainpower.

Rest – Getting adequate sleep is critical for proper brain function. There is a lot of recent research and neuroscience that explains the processes and repairs done to the brain while we sleep. That is beyond the scope of this book but know that inadequate sleep or rest will eventually cause burnout, memory loss and long-term health effects. Success does require hard work but you also have to allow the mind and body time to recover and reset itself for another round.

Caring for these three aspects of your health will allow you to operate at a peak state, which is critical to achieving massive success with SHARK Belief. Apart from learning, putting yourself in a peak state will also enhance the effectiveness of the other success elements as they work together.

The Power of Knowledge

Bill Gates and Warren Buffet are two of the richest people that have ever lived and routinely make it to the top of the list of the richest people in the world. In addition to their tremendous business success, both men are also brilliant. During a rare interview with both men, they were both asked what superpower they would pick if they could have just one. What did these men say they wanted more than anything? Both men agreed that they wanted the ability to read at super speeds! Wow, here are two men who are highly accomplished and could afford to buy anything they could ever want. They have access to the most powerful and intelligent people in the world and yet, the one superpower that Bill Gates and Warren Buffet would choose is one that caters to Knowledge. They both understand the power of knowledge and know that reading (i.e. learning) is a powerful skill to master.

Remember, it's not just about learning random facts or reading endless novels and fiction books. Gaining Knowledge is about learning and understanding specific information that will help you succeed. Knowledge is power when your learning is focused and deliberate. You must acquire knowledge that's specific to your goal and to the skills you need to build. Only then can you turn knowledge into beneficial action.

Knowledge becomes power when it guides you to act and moves you in the direction of your aim. Never stop learning, but make sure that your learning has a purpose. What you know truly matters and what you don't know may be preventing you from reaching your goal. All goals require that we have specific knowledge about what we want to accomplish.

Knowledge is paramount to success in any field and this is why it's a core element in the SHARK Belief Success Code. You may find some books or teachers focus on just one or two of the elements in SHARK Belief. It's important to remember that this is a holistic system that is most effective when all six elements play their part and work together to help you achieve success. Knowledge is power, but without a goal and the actions that will develop habits and skills, it's only potential power. Developing relationships will help you gain the knowledge you need and this knowledge will, in turn, help develop your success beliefs which will then drive you to take the action necessary to build the skills and habits that will help you reach your goals. It's all connected and works together beautifully.

CHAPTER EIGHT

Beliefs Will Change Your World

"Your beliefs become your thoughts,
Your thoughts become your words,
Your words become your actions,
Your actions become your habits,
Your habits become your values,
Your values become your destiny."
Mahatma Gandhi

Success Starts in the Mind

This is the single most important chapter in the book because it reveals to you the element that makes SHARK Belief powerful. Without this critical component, the other five areas of SHARK Belief will become inadequate and success will be difficult to attain. Belief is the element that brings it all together and is the underlying force behind the entire processes. If there were a secret to success, it would be this one area - your thoughts and your beliefs. Before you write this off as just another rehash on the Law of Attraction or some sort of New Age mystical hocus-pocus, I want to assure you that I'm referring to something much deeper and Belief is more than just mere wishing for what you really want.

Belief is all about mindset, success psychology and taking control over your mental attitude. This is not about any particular religious beliefs or your moral values, but rather, Belief is about your dominating thoughts, emotions, and attitudes. This is important because your beliefs will ultimately affect your actions and decisions. Belief is about your 'whys' and passion as well as your limiting self-doubts and fears. When I say Belief, I'm including all aspects of your mindset and referencing the use of both your conscience and subconscious mind.

If you are already familiar with the teachings of Napoleon Hill, Les Brown, Robin Sharma or Tony Robbins then you likely already understand the power of thought and will feel right at home as you read this chapter. However, if this is all new to you, then it may seem a little strange at first and will take some time before you begin to understand and believe the truths of these ideas. Nevertheless, these principles have been proven many times by practitioners in a number of fields such as psychology, marketing, professional sports, religion and medicine. I challenge you to keep an open mind and consider how your beliefs and mindset can impact your level of success.

So why are beliefs so critical to success and for reaching your goals? Because the first step to success is to believe that it's possible that you can succeed. If you don't believe in yourself, then none of the other things will matter. Every idea, dream or goal was first a seed planted in your mind. It was only after cultivating and nurturing those thoughts for a period of time that you finally decided to take action on your ideas. It starts in the mind. Reaching your goal requires personal belief in your vision and faith that you can achieve it. This must happen before you ever begin to see the results you want. You have to see it in your mind before you can see it with your eyes. You have to be willing to think big and dream big so that you can achieve big. Others will criticize your ideas and unless you have a strong belief in what you're doing, you will not be able to persevere long enough to realize your success. Strong belief is common in the sports arena and among professional athletes but this is, even more, critical when it comes to personal and business goals.

Every successful entrepreneur and innovator was once called a dreamer and told they were trying to do the impossible. It was only after their eventual success that they received praises and were labeled as geniuses. Take a look at your everyday life and realize that all of those things you see, the buildings, the planes, the companies, the books, the clothes and every technology, was first an idea in someone's mind. It's much the same with your goals and the vision for your life. Whatever you can conceive and believe, you can achieve. However, the first person you have to convince is yourself. Beyond just believing in your vision, you also have to believe in yourself. You have to believe that you are capable of doing what is necessary to get there and you also have to believe that you are worthy of the success that will accompany all that hard work.

Achieving excellence is not the result of luck or God-given talent, but rather, success is a product of who you've become through your own actions and efforts. I've discussed skills, habits, knowledge and our relationships and how they all harmonize and work together to ultimately form our environment. The combined by-product of these areas is a reflection of who we are. However, even these seemingly external elements first being in the mind and it's only after you start to change your thoughts that you will begin to see changes in your behaviors. Then, only after changing your behavior will you begin to produce the results you desire.

A Belief Defined

Essentially, a belief is an idea that you hold to be true. These ideas are impressed upon your mind beginning in early childhood. Your beliefs become true for you because they shape your perceptions, your attitudes, your feelings & moods, your assumptions & expectations and ultimately create your reality. Everything you observe happening in the world around you will get filtered through your beliefs as the images and sensory data enter your mind. Your belief filter is what creates your mindset and will play a huge role in the decisions you make and the actions you take. We all have particular beliefs about God and religion, about other people and races and most importantly, about ourselves. Our beliefs are powerful enough to compel seemingly irrational behavior and history has countless examples of people willing to die for their beliefs or ideals such as their country and their religion. When it comes down to it, your beliefs ultimately define who you are.

All of your words and actions will originate from your thoughts and you will act in accordance with what you actually believe. When it comes to achievement and excellence, your mindset will determine how high you aim, how hard you work and how much you achieve. You have to first believe in your dream or goal and then you have to believe that it's not only possible but that you are capable of succeeding. Until you adopt this frame of mind, you will never take the actions necessary to develop those areas of your life that will help you achieve your aim. Remember, we always act in a manner consistent with our deepest and most intensely held beliefs regardless of whether or not they are true.

The good news is that because every single one of your own beliefs was once learned, you can always introduce new beliefs and change your way of thinking. It may not always be easy, but it is possible to change the way you think. In one sense, your mind is like a supercomputer that can be reprogrammed and upgraded over time. Through techniques such as visualization and affirmations, you can begin to influence your subconscious mind. Actions such as writing down your goals, associating with certain people or developing your skills will reinforce beliefs, which in turn will influence your actions. It's a reinforcement loop that vacillates between action and belief with each reinforcing the other. However, this loop can work to your benefit or to your detriment depending on how you control it.

In his teaching on the power of our thoughts, Napoleon Hill emphasized that there is a difference between wishing for a thing and being ready to receive it. It's only until you really *believe* that you will be ready to receive. Hill went on to say that "the state of mind must be belief, not mere hope or wish." In other words, you first need to 'see' it and believe it, before you will be able to achieve it.

"Whether you think you can, or think you can't, you're right."

— *Henry Ford*

Beyond the Law of Attraction

Before I go deeper into why your thoughts and beliefs play a significant role in your success, I want to preface these thoughts with an important point. Beyond a success-oriented mindset, achieving excellence requires that you take action. It's important that you remember this fact throughout this chapter because I see far too many people get excited about the power of the mind only stop after they make their vision boards and recite affirmations. Don't just visualize and then go about your day as usual. You have to execute! Achieving success means that you take massive action to get you moving in the direction you want to go. It's only after you step out and take action that you find that yourself "attracting" opportunities into your life. It's only when you actually go out and talk to people that you meet just the right person. It's only after you begin working on new skills and habits that you catch that "lucky break." Without action, the Law of Attraction falls short.

So what is this philosophy called the "Law of Attraction?" It has actually been around for thousands of years but only in recent times has it gone by this name. Essentially, it states that you are a "living magnet" and will attract into your life that which you think about the most. It says that "like attracts like" and that you will attract to into your life the people, ideas, opportunities or circumstances that align with your dominant thoughts and words.

In the mid-2000's, there was a very popular (and controversial) book & movie about the Law of Attraction that took the world by storm called *The Secret*. It claimed that the universe is governed by a universal 'law' which has the power to create life-changing results such as increased happiness, health, and wealth. Though these ideas had been written about many times in the past, this new take was immensely popular and went on to sell tens of millions of books in just a few short years. However, all that fame also brought with it the critics. They argued that *The Secret* gave people false hope and that people couldn't just think their way to success. The critics also argued that there was no proof for this "law" and was more of a gimmick than it was a valid technique for attaining success.

I personally witnessed many aspiring entrepreneurs and sales professionals become inspired by *The Secret* only to give up a few months later and join the ranks of those that said it didn't work. Regardless, the power of positive thinking and the ideas surrounding the law of attraction have been around for a long time and millions of people have attended seminars and read books to learn more about how to attract the things they want into their lives. Like most things, you will find both supporters and critics.

My point is not to argue for or against the merits of using the Law of Attraction. I have studied it quite a bit over the years and have observed its benefits as well as its limitations. Through the use of tools and techniques such as creating vision boards and using visualization methods, one can have even more success in reaching a goal. However, I have also realized that when someone tries to use the Law of Attraction as a stand-alone method, it usually leads to failure and disappointment. Why? Because excellence is the byproduct of massive action! Belief is often the spark that gets you started and is also the fuel that keeps you persevering. However, it is ultimately the daily grind that yields results.

The power of Belief lies in the activity it drives you to engage in. It's found in the decisions you make and your reaction to everyday situations. I'm repetitive here but only because it's critical that you understand this. Beyond the Law of Attraction, vision boards, and affirmations, you need to take *massive action* and do everything in your power to begin making your vision a reality. Even the New Testament book of James notes this important point when it says, "faith without deeds, is dead." You can claim to believe in something and convince yourself that you will get what you desire, but until you actually go out there and make something happen, nothing will ever come of your thoughts. Take action, or you will have little more than dead faith.

Don't get me wrong, I am a huge believer in the power of one's thoughts and the use of positive affirmations, but success, great health or awesome relationships always require a great deal more than just dreaming about them. If you want to actually attract something in your life, then you need to work on *becoming* the person that attracts those things. The only way to become a new person is through change and personal change means doing new things. At the end of the day, it's all about action! This is the ongoing loop I described in the first part of this chapter. You start with some belief about your goal and then take action towards it. That action then reinforces or changes your beliefs, which then drives more actions and so forth. Engaging in both action and belief keeps you moving in the right direction. Now that we're clear on this point let's get back to focusing on the power of the mind and its impact on our success.

Thoughts Are Things

Your mind is very much like a camera, in that it gathers input from the outside world, but is also much like a projector in that it will interpret those inputs and create new meaning from every situation in the form of images that you remember. We see this time again when we analyze two people that observe the same situation and one will see a disaster while the other sees opportunity. Those two people will see the same thing and yet they will interpret it entirely differently, driving each one to completely different emotions and reactions. Such is the power of your imagination!

Through the use of your imagination, you also have the power to dream up visions of your ideal future, brainstorm solutions to your problems, and create new ideas. Your mind is the central hub of the

SHARK Belief Success Code and each of the other elements are like spokes that go out from this center to create the wheel that carries you to success. It all has to start in the mind. You will never define an aim, establish new habits, develop new skills or build new relationships unless you can first see yourself doing those things. This is the process that turns thoughts into reality. First comes a thought, which then grows into an idea and desire. Finally, it becomes a concrete plan to take the first step and ultimately manifests itself in action.

Napoleon Hill wrote that the starting point of all achievement is to first develop a burning desire for what you want. This is because you will ultimately manifest into existence what you think about the most. Not just through your thoughts alone of course, but through the eventual words and actions taken as a result of those ideas growing in your mind. Your dominating thoughts and ideas soon become a sort of obsession, which then drives you to make the plans necessary to achieve it. Remember, everything mankind has ever created first originated as an idea. It began as a thought in someone's mind and then manifested itself into its physical form. Every invention, building, and the organization were the result of the creative process that took place in a person's mind.

Let's examine this as it relates to SHARK Belief. Think about a major goal you've set for yourself. Where did that goal and desire to achieve it come from? It originated as an idea planted in your mind! Once you have this idea, you begin to nurture and cultivate it and it begins to grow bigger and more powerful. You'll think about it for days or months until you become almost obsessive about it. Then, when you are convinced and believe, do you decided to set a goal for yourself to achieve that aim and thus begins the process of taking action. Perhaps you start by reaching out to other like-minded individuals to learn more about the skills & knowledge required for your goal. Perhaps you change some habits or put new routines into place. All of this because you had an idea. Thoughts truly become things!

Any thought nurtured in this way will eventually begin to manifest itself in its physical form. As a result of your mental focus, your thoughts will be in tune with what you want and you'll begin to notice things you hadn't before. You'll see opportunities or find information that can help you. Your burning desire will start to turn your thoughts into things the moment you begin to take action by transforming those ideas into words & actions. It's important to notice that this requires you to have a *burning desire*. To be successful, your idea has to be more than just a vaguely expressed wish. It has to become a desire strong enough to produce in you the success consciousness that gives you the confidence and determination to take action. A burning desire provides you with the fortitude you'll need to persevere until you see your ideas become reality. This is important because even when you begin taking action, you may not see the results right away. A burning desire for the vision you created in your imagination will help keep you going. Success always begins with a state of mind.

The human mind is more powerful than most people realize. Your thoughts are so powerful they can even make physical changes to your body. We often see examples of this during pharmaceutical or medical testing. It's amazing to see the body healed simply as the result of a person thinking they've been given the medicine that can cure them. For example, during drug testing, one group gets the real drug designed to cure a particular illness while another group takes a sugar pill that they think is actual medication. Yet, we see people in both groups get healed! We've seen this same healing effect with "placebo surgeries" and other non-traditional medicines. The placebo effect is a powerful example of just how real our thoughts are.

Just as your thoughts have the power to change your heart rate or heal the body, they also have the power to create your reality by changing your outlook on life and influencing your behavior. Your mindset is so powerful and plays such a big role in your success that neglecting this one area can undo all of the hard work you put into the other five elements of SHARK Belief. Professional athletes and sports teams have known this for a long time which is why they constantly encourage one another and stay positive during competitions. How much more important is it for us to take this same approach in our own personal and business lives?

Napoleon Hill was way ahead of his time when he realized that thoughts are things. Neuroscience has since proven that a person's thoughts will literally create electrical impulses in the brain which have even been used to control bionic limbs and send electrical signals. Beyond just creating electrical brain impulses, Hill noted that our mind is much like a radio transmitter and receiver. In addition to receiving ideas, our thoughts are also *projected* out and if repeatedly done, they will begin to manifest themselves into their physical equivalents. That's an incredible idea and may be difficult to comprehend but our minds are far more powerful than most people realize! If thoughts are things, then we must maximize this truth and use it to help us reach our goals rather than to bring about our fears. Your thoughts have the power to create as well as the power to destroy. It all comes down to which thoughts you choose to give life to and nurture.

Choose Your Thoughts Carefully

Have you ever wondered where your ideas come from? Are the majority of our ideas the result of our own creativity or are they simply a product of the countless sensory inputs that feed our minds? The truth is, most of your ideas are not original thoughts but rather they are byproducts of the things you've seen and heard. If thoughts are things and they have the power to create our realities, then it's critical that we guard our minds against negative or destructive thoughts. In today's world of media saturation, we are constantly being bombarded with content and images, all of which are competing for our attention and ultimately for their share of influence in our lives. Advertisers spend billions of dollars every year because they know that their influence will drive your purchasing decisions.

Our minds are easily susceptible to outside influences so it's critical that we maintain a constant awareness of the things influencing our thoughts and beliefs. Though we have to balance this by keeping an open mind to new ideas that could help us grow and reach our goals, we must always be on guard for those negative ideas which result in fear, doubt, and limiting beliefs, so that we can quickly dismiss them and prevent them from taking root.

Did you know that the movies you watch, the music you listen to and the news you read all have a slow and subtle way of reprogramming your mind and changing your views of the world? This is not an exaggeration! Let's take a common example and look at the stereotypical businessman depicted in today's movies. They are usually coldhearted, corrupt, greedy and selfish individuals that have gained money and power while sacrificing their marriages and family. Hollywood loves to portray the extreme cases of business people because it sells movies. You will be hard pressed to find movies depicting the hard working entrepreneur that is making a difference in the world while also living modestly and making quality time for their family and community. However, it is the latter example that is most common and it's usually people with these positive character traits that are making the most difference in the world and achieving the most success. Many of us have been programmed to think that all successful business-types are like the ones we see in the movies, so we end up adopting limiting beliefs about what it takes to be a successful entrepreneur or what it means to be financially well off. Many people see money and wealth as evil things. Consequently, those same people will never have financial abundance in their own lives.

I use this example to show how something as subtle as a fictional movie character can influence our thinking and beliefs. The same holds true for music, the people we work with, our teachers, parents, books and even the comments posted on social media. They all influence our thinking and because of our built-in primal survival mechanisms, we are compelled to want to fit in with the tribe. Fitting in with the tribe means survival. Unfortunately, fitting in with the tribe also means accepting how the masses think and adopting their worldview. This can have a detrimental effect on your thoughts since much of the media is dramatized fiction and highly opinionated information being spread by those with an agenda that's not always congruent with your goals or desires.

We all like to believe that our thoughts are our own and that we do our own thinking. The reality is that very little of your thoughts were your own ideas and most of your opinions are the byproducts of the information you consume and the beliefs you've adopted. I'm not claiming that this is good or bad. I'm just pointing out how the mind works so that you can use it to your advantage.

Much like training and strengthening a muscle in your leg, your thought-control and creative muscles can also be developed. Once you begin to get into the habit of paying attention to what influences you, you'll find it easier to control your thoughts. Additionally, thinking of new ideas and becoming more creative is also a skill you can develop with practice. Get into the habit of using your imagination to think of new ideas, new solutions and new ways to add value. You'll soon find yourself thinking of new ideas all the time as your creative muscles develop.

To reach the highest levels of achievement, one thing you will need to do is begin guarding your thoughts against negative influences and controlling what feeds your mind. It's certainly not easy to do with all the distractions available to us today but you must make a deliberate effort if you are to have any shot at achieving what you set out to do. I personally make it a habit of listening to a few minutes of motivational speeches every day and will regularly read books and articles on personal development. I read quotes about success and perseverance. I hang around people that are thinking big and have a success mindset because I know that their way of thinking will rub off on me. I also limit the time I spend listening to celebrity gossip or reading the headline news. Most of it is pretty depressing or fear-based anyway. I find that I am much happier now! I do all of this because I know it all has a positive influence on my mind and I've learned the importance of managing one's psychology. **Success requires self-control, and self-control is the result of thought-control. Always remember that you have the power to think, and more importantly, you have the power to control your thoughts.** Make use of this power by controlling your thoughts to transform yourself into the person you need to become to reach your goals.

We all have to face adversity and challenges in life. Many times, we're impacted by things entirely out of our control but at the end of the day, we still have the power to choose how will react to them. We choose how we will view failures and challenges. We determine the mental attitude we will have about our past and about our future.

You Become What You Think About

If you want to change your life, then it starts by changing how you think. You don't begin to change your life by changing how you dress or upgrading the car you drive. Rather, you start changing your life by changing your beliefs and changing your state of mind. The conversations you have with yourself in your mind will reveal themselves through how you speak and act. If you constantly think about self-doubt, fear and failure, then you'll find yourself pointing out the reasons why something won't work or why you can't do it. However, if you think of yourself as confident and optimistic, then you'll be more likely to act on the opportunities you see and more likely to take the steps necessary to grow as an individual.

In his audio classic titled *The Strangest Secret*, Earl Nightingale discusses why some men become financially successful while the vast majority of others do not. He makes a potent argument for the fact that most people just don't think about becoming successful or put a deliberate effort into learning how to become financially well off. The value of this speech is not in that Nightingale discusses a 'how-to' approach to becoming wealthy, but rather he goes into the power of the mind to change one's circumstances. He emphasized the notion that, 'You will become that which you think about the most.'

Below is one of my favorite excerpts from his speech:

"People do what they make up their minds to do. So get rid of the ancient superstition once and for all that people who earn big money are special people, or lucky, or get the breaks or had money to begin with, or knew someone, or are smarter, or anything else. These are alibis, and they can all be disproved a thousand times. The reason there are so many of these alibis around is that men who fail to make the grade financially are seldom honest enough to just admit that they really didn't try and keep trying. So to justify their failure, in order to remain seated, they dream up and pass along these old alibis. **We're all self-made, but only the successful will admit it.**"

We're all self-made! These are potent words, and you can either say 'Amen' or 'Ouch.' Most people never see the hard work, the sacrifice and the time it took for someone to become financially successful. By the time anyone reaches that point, the only thing that other people notice is their nice stuff, their expensive vacations and the lifestyle they can now afford. It is only then that they look and say, "Wow, they were just born lucky."

Now, we all know that ideas alone won't make you rich since you also have to act on them. Success takes hustle, hard work, and patience. But success always starts with an idea and developing the habit of continually finding new ways to add value, solve problems and enrich others will put you miles ahead of most people. Nightingale makes this point clear when he says, "No man can get rich himself unless he enriches others."

"Human beings can alter their lives by altering their attitude of mind. It's another way of saying, '**We become what we think about**.'" Those six words have the power to transform a life when fully understood. You have now realized that success with SHARK

Belief requires more than just thinking about it, it takes action. However, you also know that success starts in the mind and before you begin taking action, you must first believe that it's possible.

Focus on What You Want

I have a couple of friends who are avid cyclists and ride their bikes almost every day. The first time they invited me to go mountain bike riding with them along the desert hills in sunny Arizona, my friend Ric was kind enough to give me some words of wisdom for the ride ahead. He said to me, "Look at where you want the bike to go and not at what you wish to avoid." You see, these dirt trails were lined with sharp rocks, cactus, steep ledges and some other desert features that could become quite hazardous if crashed into at high speeds. Like any rational person, I wanted to avoid any serious bodily harm that could come from this ride and he must have noticed the slight nervousness in my face.

While riding a mountain bike, it's pretty easy to avoid the hazards if you maintain a slow speed but there's no fun in that. When riding, things get pretty fast and the slightest movement of your body can mean the difference between successfully making it around a tight curve and crashing into the sides of the trail. It takes an intense focus to navigate those winding trails because your body will subconsciously steer the bike where your head and eyes are pointed. That is why Ric told me it was best to focus on the trail ahead and not on the pitfalls I wanted to avoid. I didn't ignore the hazards alongside the trail altogether, but rather I devoted the majority of my attention to focusing on the path ahead and spending only a tiny bit of my peripheral attention to staying aware of the dangers. The important thing is that most of my mental energy went to staying focused on where I wanted to go.

After the ride, I realized that this wisdom could also be applied to many areas of life and is especially important for our goals and business success. You have to direct the majority of your attention to focusing on what you want and where you wish to go as opposed to focusing on what you don't want. If you dwell on the pitfalls and constantly worry about everything that can go wrong, then like a self-fulfilling prophecy, you'll find that a lot of things will go wrong! It's what the Law of Attraction teaches and unfortunately, too many people use this in reverse by engaging their minds in constant fear and worry. Then when things go wrong, they say "see, I knew that would happen to me!"

Just to be clear, I'm not telling you to stick your head in the sand to avoid addressing real threats to your goals or business, because any wise person will keep tabs on potential risks and look for ways to mitigate them. However, there is an enormous difference between someone that understands the potential risks and someone that dwells on them fearfully. This is about avoiding the latter.

It's far too easy to let a small worry turn into constant fear of failure. Before you know it, your imagination runs wild with images of the worst-case scenario playing out over and over. You have to be mindful of this kind of thinking and immediately break that train of thought by replacing the images of fear and disaster with those of success and desired outcomes. As Les Brown put it, "What you focus on the longest, becomes the strongest." You CAN take control of your thoughts. While it may not always be easy, it's absolutely necessary.

Empowering Beliefs vs. Limiting Beliefs

The Bugatti Veyron is one of the fastest road legal production cars in the world. This incredible machine boasts a top speed of over 400 km/hr and can accelerate from 0 to 100 km/hr in under three seconds!

It was made for attaining incredible speed and has all of the capabilities to do so. Nothing is holding this car back except for the driver's choice to go slower. Contrast the Bugatti to the production cars built by BMW, Audi, and Mercedes-Benz. While they also manufacture beautiful and powerful automobiles, the vast majority of their cars are produced with a governor, or limiter, that restricts the vehicles from exceeding speeds of 250 km/hr. These electronic limiters restrict the cars from accelerating beyond a certain speed, even if the cars are physically capable of doing so. The limiter creates an artificial ceiling on how fast the driver can make the car go.

There are two basic belief types and one is much like the governor device on the automobiles we just compared; these are *empowering beliefs* and *limiting beliefs*. Empowering beliefs will propel you and carry you to your fullest potential while limiting beliefs will put a ceiling on the level of success you attain. Most people have incredible potential and are capable of achieving amazing things with their lives, but because of limiting beliefs, they are often contained to levels of excellence that are far short of their true capabilities.

Empowering beliefs are those that are conducive to creating the success you want. Remember that much of our reality is created by the perceptions in our mind. To be successful, you have to transform your thinking into a success mindset. You must have a growth mindset rather than a fixed and restricted mindset. Sometimes, this requires challenging your current beliefs about certain things and changing the way you view them. When it comes to achieving excellence, much of your success will be attributed to how you view things such as failure, criticism, rejection, personal development, discipline, hard work and the all traits required for excellence.

The following section highlights some limiting beliefs that must be conquered as well as some awesome empowering beliefs that should be adopted before great achievements can be made.

Excuses

In his book *The Magic of Thinking Big*, David Schwartz coined the term "excuse-itis" which he uses to describe someone that has an excuse for everything. Those that have failed or have yet to start pursuing their goals will typically have a major case of excuse-itis. They make an excuse for everything and every failure is because of someone else. They claim to be too old, or too young, or too broke, or too busy or they say they don't have enough education or enough skill or that they're not smart enough and that the economy is bad. These are all just limiting beliefs and the list can go on forever. This is a dream killer and if you recognize this attitude in your life, begin to change it by taking immediate action and utilizing the techniques in this chapter. Take action to start reprograming your mind. Action is the best antidote for excuse-itis. Quit making excuses for why you can't do something and use that mental energy to figure out *how* you can.

Fear

Fear is the biggest culprit for why most people don't succeed and is often why people fail to get started. Fear is a powerful enemy that will paralyze you if you let it dominate your mind. Fears such as the Fear of Criticism, the Fear of Failure, the Fear of Being Wrong and the Fear of Rejection have been responsible for more people remaining in poverty than has any economic recession or famine. Fear breeds worry and while both are just states of mind, they soon become habits that can control our lives. Fear is a very real issue in our lives and we must begin to fight it or we'll never reach our fullest potential. The subject of fear is of such importance that Napoleon Hill devoted an entire chapter to it in his classic *Think and Grow Rich*. In a chapter he titled *The Six Ghosts of Fear*, he outlines some ways that we can analyze our fears as well as proven ways to conquer them. We all face fears in life and have to deal with it, but it comes down to how we respond to fear. It's okay to feel a little afraid, nervous or cautious in new situations, just don't let fear rule your mind.

One of my favorite acronyms for the definition of F.E.A.R. is False Evidence Appearing Real. It points to the fact that our fears are created in the mind, are a by-product of our imagination and exist only in our thoughts about the future. Our fears are often about things or situations that do not currently exist and may never become a reality. While dangers and risks themselves are very real, the emotion of fear is a by-product of how we choose to interpret and react to those situations. Fear is a natural reaction to things we believe to be a threat. We may never be able to completely eliminate the emotions of fear, but we do have the power to overcome our fears and press on in spite of them. It's okay to feel fear, just don't surrender to it. The greatest antidote to fear is action. It is often the things we are most afraid of doing that we most need to do.

Failure

Because of the traditional school system and the way most of us were raised, we tend to see failure in a very negative view. If we got the answer wrong, we failed the test. If we failed to meet deadlines or follow the rules, we were chastised and disciplined without explanation. If we lost a game, we were ridiculed and told we could never win. Most people see failure as a bad thing and as a sign, they are not cut out to achieve great things. I'm not suggesting that we should all want to fail, but rather that we should change our attitudes toward failure. Failure and temporary defeats are a part of life and can help us grow. We should see them as lessons and opportunities to try again rather than as reasons to quit. We should seek to improve after each failure instead of looking for ways to avoid doing things we've failed at in the past.

Self-Efficacy & Confidence

Self-efficacy is a term psychologists use to describe a person's belief in their ability to affect situations. Your beliefs about your ability to influence specific situations will play a significant role in how you approach goals and challenges. If you believe everything is out of your control, that life happens and there is nothing you can do to change things, then you are said to have low self-efficacy. This is not the same as self-esteem and has little to do with accepting or liking yourself. It's about your point of view regarding your power to influence outcomes, develop new skills and shape your life's course.

Self-efficacy is about having that "can do" attitude versus embracing the "it is what it is" approach to life. People with high self-efficacy believe that they can direct more areas of their lives and shape the outcomes of situations and as a result, they often do. This empowering belief is at the core of this entire chapter and I'm hoping by now, you have realized just how much control you have over your thoughts as well as traits such as skills, knowledge, and habits.

"Destiny is not a matter of chance, it is a matter of choice.
It is not a thing to be waited for, it is a thing to be achieved."
- William Jennings Bryan

Below is a list of seven empowering beliefs that you should consider making your own.

1. I don't have to be great to get started, but I have to get started to be great.
2. I have a never-ending amount of possibilities at my fingertips.
3. I have the power to create new things and new experiences.
4. Failure is just a lesson and challenges make me stronger.
5. The past is behind me and my present & future life are even better.
6. Success is the result of working hard & working smart and does not come from luck or God-given talent.
7. I have the power to grow as a person and transform my life, my body, and my mind.

Reprogramming Your Mind

You can slowly begin to reprogram your mind over time through repetition. It is very similar to developing a new skill or building a new habit. The more often that you practice these techniques and the more deliberate you are when doing them, the quicker you'll begin to change your thinking. When it comes to influencing your thoughts, techniques such as visualization, auto-suggestion and affirmations are just as compelling as reading books, watching a video or talking with other people.

Watch your words! To cultivate empowering beliefs, one of the first things we need to do is begin changing our vocabulary. These are subtle changes and there are several key words and phrases that you should completely eliminate from your daily dialogue. Start by replacing phrases such as "I can't do that", "that's impossible" and "I've never been good at this" with phrases such as "How can I achieve that", "there is always a way" and "It's never too late to learn and improve my skills".

You see, the first set of phrases are negative and limiting while the second set opens up possibilities and challenge you to expand your thinking, discover solutions and seek personal growth. There are a lot of words that we've used for a long time that are negative and usually just said out of habit now. You should stop yourself when you start saying things like "this always happens to me," "it's so hard," or "how annoying". Your words are a reflection of your thoughts and negative words have just as much power as positive affirmations to program your thinking. It's very subtle but over time, this small change can make a huge difference in your ability to excel in life.

Positive Affirmations

It's important to monitor your self-talk and begin using positive affirmations. Say things such as "I'm am learning to…", "I'm am good at and getter better at…", "I believe in myself", "I am capable of…", "My ability to conquer my challenges is limitless; my potential to succeed is infinite.", "I am (courageous, confident, friendly, _____ fill in the blank)". Positive affirmations begin to seep into the subconscious mind and will start to change your beliefs.

Visualization

At the 2008 Beijing Olympics, Michael Phelps made history by winning eight gold medals, resulting in the most first-place finishes at any single Olympic Games. Phelps began swimming at age seven and with the help of his coach, Bob Bowman, he became one of the greatest swimming champions of all time. Bowman trained Phelps to master all of the physical techniques and conditioning needed to succeed, but he also gave Phelps a secret weapon that would give him an edge over other swimmers and one that would make all the difference during the Olympics. Bowman knew that in addition to incredible physical traits, a champion also needed the right mindset. The weapon he gave Phelps was mental visualization.

In his book *The Power of Habit*, Charles Duhigg writes of the visualization training Coach Bowman instructed Phelps to perform.

"When Phelps was a teenager, for instance, at the end of each practice, Bowman would tell him to go home and 'watch the videotape. Watch it before you go to sleep and when you wake up.'

The videotape wasn't real. Rather it was a mental visualization of the perfect race. Each night before falling asleep and each morning after waking up, Phelps would imagine himself jumping off the blocks and, in slow motion, swimming flawlessly. He would visualize his strokes, the walls of the pool, his turns, and the finish. He would imagine the wake behind his body, the water dripping off his lips as his mouth cleared the surface, what it would feel like to rip off his cap at the end. He would lie in bed with his eyes shut and watch the entire competition, the smallest details, again and again, until he knew each second by heart."

During the 2008 Olympics, this visualization training made the difference in Phelps winning eight gold medals. In one particular race where Phelps's swimming goggles malfunctioned, he switched on the 'videotape' and used it to guide him through the remainder of the race. He won another gold. After the race, a reporter asked what it felt like to swim blind and Phelps replied, "It felt like I imagined it would." Wow, just like he had imagined! The flawless race he had played in his mind over and over had become a reality.

Professional athletes have long known about the power of visualization and the effects it has on the mind to influence the outcome of competitions. While this technique is common in the sports world, for some reason it's still an uncommon practice in the business community. When we were children, we used our imaginations all the time as we played and pretended that we were our favorite cartoon characters. We used our imaginations when we played with a simple toy and created vast worlds... all in our mind.

Visualization is very much like how you used your imagination as a child. However, in this case, you are imagining your future self and seeing yourself achieve the success you desire. If you have an idea of what you want and what it will look like when you achieve your goal, then you can use visualization to help you reach your goal. Imagine what it will look like when you launch your first product or service, imagine what it will feel like when you make that sale or when you give that speech. Imagine yourself receiving that award or cashing that check. What does it look like, what are the sounds you'll hear, what does it smell like, feel like, what emotions will you experience? The more detailed your videotape, the more powerful and effective your visualization will be.

The reason visualization is so powerful is because your subconscious mind and nervous system cannot tell the difference between a real experience and an imagined one. Especially when that imagined experience is supercharged with positive emotions. This is easily demonstrated when a person has a nightmare and wakes from their dream only to find their heart pounding and their pillow covered in sweat. They weren't actually engaged in the physical experience but their minds thought they were and so it created a physiological response in the body. This same effect can be used to produce good things in our lives and to help us change our beliefs.

If you're having a hard time believing that you can actually accomplish the goal you've set out for yourself, then visualization can help by letting you 'see yourself' doing it. Often times, we won't believe something until we first see it. By engaging in regular visualization, you are creating *practice experiences* and reinforcing your beliefs every time you do so. Much like building a new habit, the power of visualization is in the repetition. The mind can be reprogrammed and this is done over time through repeating the same thoughts and affirmations. By visualizing yourself accomplishing that goal and imagining the good feelings and sights that come with achievement, you are slowing changing your beliefs. It is through doing this that you will begin to believe that you can and will achieve success.

"Your imagination is your preview of life's coming attractions"
- Albert Einstein

Here is a simple way to engage in effective visualization. It can be done in as little as five minutes each day and the more consistently you do it, the more powerful it will become.

1. Find a place where you can close your eyes and relax undisturbed for a few minutes.
2. Close your eyes and begin by taking in a deep breath and slowly exhaling. Do this for one minute and begin to forget about what you were just doing. This helps you relax and clears your mind first.
3. Next, think of a time when you succeeded or experienced the feelings of achievement, confidence, and happiness. Remember those feelings and briefly, relive that moment. Doing this will help you link positive emotions to the future-self you are about to visualize.
4. Now, imagine that you have just reached your goal. Imagine your future self and go into as much detail as possible. Make

it a full-body experience and get all of your senses involved. You want to imagine and experience this moment as if you are actually living it. What does this moment look like? Where are you and who's there with you? What do you look like and how are you acting? What sights, sounds, and smells are you experiencing? What feelings and emotions do you have? Point out the slightest details. It's important to make sure your mental picture is as vivid and detailed as possible so that it begins to permeate your subconscious mind. Play pretend just like you did as a child.

5. When you're done with the visualization, open your eyes, take in a deep breath and smile. Project feelings of gratitude and confidence that you will achieve your goal.

Think Big

One of my favorite sculptures is Auguste Rodin's, *The Thinker*. The work shows a male figure sitting on a rock with his chin resting on one hand as though deep in thought. This sculpture is often used as an image to represent intellect or philosophy. Every time I see it, I can't help but wonder what he's been thinking about all this time. My imagination conjures up images of Big Thinking, profound philosophical arguments, and world-changing ideas. I've have always enjoyed learning new things, reading books, challenging my mind and in general, just thinking. I don't mind being alone at times because it gives me a quiet time to think and focus my mental energy. I love exploring new ideas and using my imagination to create new thoughts and mental images. I even have a sign in my office that reads "Think Big!" to serve as a reminder.

I honestly believe it is big thinking that propels the world forward and ideas that are just beyond the realm of possibility will eventually become reality. Just look at how new technology often resembles the ideas first seen in Science Fiction. Big ideas create excitement and motivation and will attract the people and resources necessary to pursue those ideas.

If you want to accomplish big things in life, then you need to think big and dream big. You need to set big goals and believe big. However, an important lesson I've learned is that all of my great ideas and newfound knowledge will do me no good unless I take action. I have realized that while the mind is incredibly powerful, it is still my day-to-day actions and habits that will transform lives and accomplish big things. Unlike Rodin's Thinker, we can't just sit around all day thinking of new ideas. Execution is the name of the game and we need to act. Your action can be a tiny step forward or a huge leap of faith, but either way, you must act. Think big, but always remember that until you take action, you'll be just like Rodin's *Thinker*, ever pondering. Eventually, we all need to get off that rock and take the first step.

Begin with Belief

To accomplish great things in life, you must start to cultivate a success consciousness and a mindset that is favorable to producing excellence. Within the SHARK Belief context, Belief is that powerful force from which all of the other elements in the process hinge and are made useful. You must believe that you can reach your goals. You must believe that you are capable of developing new skills and acquiring useful knowledge. You must believe that you have the capacity to change and direct the outcomes of your life. You must believe that fundamental relationships will make a difference to your success. You must believe that success is the result of hard work, passion, and discipline rather than lucky breaks. You must believe that thoughts are things and that success always begins with a state of mind. You must believe in your dream and you must believe in yourself. *Beliefs* will change your world.

Put Your Mind to It

Growing up, I often heard well-meaning parents and teachers use the phrase "you can do anything you set your mind to." Hearing that phrase would often inspire me to try harder or it would somehow give me hope for accomplishing great things in my life. However, as much as I liked to hear it and as much as I agreed with it, I really didn't know what it meant or how to apply it to my life. What exactly does "put your mind to it" mean? Does it mean that I need to learn more and apply my intellect to achieve the results I want? Does it mean that if I just think about it a lot, eventually my dreams will come to pass? Is this phrase about focus? Perhaps it means using Jedi-like mind power to perform feats such as moving the immovable and convincing the otherwise stubborn. Since embarking on my journey to discover what makes someone successful and through the processes of arriving at the SHARK Belief elements, I have since learned a tremendous amount of what it really means to put your mind to something.

By now, you also have insight into the various elements of SHARK Belief and you have seen the importance of mindset and the battles that take place inside your head. All six of these elements hinge on some area of your mind, the physical brain or your emotions. Putting your mind to something means so much more than just thinking or wishing for it. It means more than just learning about that something. It means more than having mental fortitude and persistence.

While these may be necessary traits, putting your mind to something requires a holistic approach that engages every aspect of your being necessary to align you with the processes that will take you to your goal. It means using all six of the SHARK Belief elements in harmony with one another to change who and what you are to attract the success you desire. This includes everything from your beliefs to your skills, habits and even your relationships. You really can do anything that you put your mind to, you just need to know what it means to "put your mind to it" and begin the process of doing that which is necessary.

This chapter, and, more importantly, this entire book, gives you the blueprint needed to start pursuing that which you desire. You now have an understanding of what those common elements of success are and how to begin using them in your own life. You now have the tools to start working towards your goal. You just need to put your mind to it!

CHAPTER NINE

Getting Started with SHARK Belief

Congratulations! You now have an understanding of the six elements and why they're critical for success. Let's look at a quick review of the entire formula. We started with Aim because until you know where you're going, you'll never get there. Success must have a clear goal and end result. Your first step is to define exactly what it is that you want to accomplish. You don't necessarily need to know *how* you will get there, but you certainly need a vision for what your success looks like. The more concrete and narrow that is, the easier it will be to begin applying the other elements. After you've set your Aim, you can then begin constructing a plan for getting there and this is where Skills, Habits, Relationships and Knowledge come in.

To achieve your Aim, you will need to develop and use particular skills or techniques that are specific to what you want to accomplish. Depending on your goal, you may need a lot of skills or just one or two simple techniques. Remember, a good way to bridge gaps in your skills may be by working with other people that have the skills you need. Not all skills can be bridged this way but many technical and knowledge based skills can be. If you're not sure what skills are needed, then start by gaining more knowledge that is specific to your goal. Having deep domain expertise on what you want to accomplish will make you more successful, but you must develop this while also taking action. Don't wait until you feel that you "know enough." There is a variety of ways to accomplish this but the easiest ways are doing your own research online and by connecting with someone that's already achieved what you want to do.

If you're not sure where to start, then learning from others is the fastest way to shorten your learning curve and building key relationships will go far beyond the passing of knowledge and information. Key relationships will also influence your beliefs and convictions about your goal. If you see that others have already done it, your resolve will increase which will help keep you motivated. There are several other key relationships you need to build to continue making progress such as mentors, coaches, and mastermind groups. You must also be aware of negative relationships that are having a detrimental impact on your growth. Limit those as much as possible.

Finally, habits are what will keep you making consistent and daily progress. You won't always feel like doing what you need to do so creating a routine will help keep you more organized and consistent. Just like exercising, powerful results don't appear after one or two big workouts but are instead the product of a dedication over the long-term. Don't underestimate the power of taking small and consistent action. Habits rule our lives and we must understand them and use them to our advantage. Implement habits that complement the other elements such as skill building, relationship building or gaining new knowledge.

Beliefs permeate and connect all of these elements together. Your success will require a specific mindset and this area is entirely in your control. Along with mental activity such as visualization and affirmations, you must also be on guard for limiting beliefs such as fear and doubt. Success is as much mental as it is physical so never underestimate the power of your thoughts. Begin to reprogram your mind so you can become more positive and success oriented. That incredible machinery between your ears can be continually upgraded and reprogrammed to do your bidding. Your thoughts drive your words and actions and they are what ultimately yield the results you want.

While each one of these elements is powerful all by itself, the synergistic effect of all six working in harmony simultaneously has the power to take an ordinary person and help them accomplish the extraordinary. The six elements reinforce each other and begin moveing you toward your goal at increasing rates. Depending on your goal, you may require more of some of the elements than others, but at some level, ALL SIX are still needed for success in anything. Neglect one or more of them and you will begin to limit the results and progress you'll see.

It's Up To You

As I've stated repeatedly, all of this information will be nothing more than idle potential until you begin taking action. This is both the good news and the bad news. The level of success that you want to reach in life depends ENTIRELY ON YOU AND ONLY YOU. I know it's a cliché but it's true. You can lead a horse to water but you can't make it drink. At the end of the day, this is your life and you are responsible for it. Not your parents, your spouse, best friend, and business partner or your mentor. Just you. There is no savior on a white horse coming to rescue you. There are no chariots or magic carpets that will take you to paradise and make all of your dreams and wishes come true. You are not going to win the lottery. The government is not going to rescue you and all those promises the next politician makes will be forgotten. Opportunity will not come knocking on your door. You've got to make it happen.

I'm really trying to hammer this point home so let me try that again… It's ALL UP TO YOU! That can be a scary thought but it's also very liberating. One of life's greatest gifts is freedom. You have the freedom to think the thoughts you want, the freedom to choose your goals and the freedom to change the direction of your life. If you live in a modern and open society, then you have no excuses. The sooner you get over the excuses for why you haven't been successful or why you can't do something, the sooner you'll begin to see progress. It's no one else's fault. Success is your responsibility and your life is in your own hands. Accept that and make the most of it by taking action. I see a lot well-meaning people engage in "shelf-help". They buy the books or workshops and after they get through it, they're put on the bookshelf to collect dust. The ideas are never implemented and off that person goes looking for the next new thing. Please don't let this be just another book you get through and never come back to once you're done. The ideas here are meant to be revisited and referenced often along your journey. Use SHARK Belief as your map.

Getting Started

The SHARK Belief Success Code consolidates quite a bit of information and tactics into six major elements. However, even six areas can become overwhelming and you may not be sure how to plan your approach or how to get started. There are two tools that I've used which will help you get started. The first one helps you plan how you will use SHARK Belief and the second helps you keep momentum and track progress.

Plan It! - The SHARK Belief Success Map

I always begin by making a SHARK Belief Success Map. You can do this on a whiteboard, a piece of paper or even on the notes within your phone. This map serves as a way to think through the elements and plan your approach. It's only a way to get started and you'll soon realize that once you've started taking action, you'll see more of the path ahead and will need to adjust some of these initial thoughts. The SHARK Belief Success Map works by answering questions about what you want to accomplish and helping you determine you first step.

A – Aim

Start with Aim and answer the following questions:

- What is my goal and what will it look like when I achieve it?
- When would I like to accomplish this by?

After you have your goal defined, answer the questions below for each of the following four elements. You do not need to do this in any particular order but I have found that starting with Knowledge or Relationships is often the best place.

S – Skills

- Which skills or techniques are essential for accomplishing this goal? (List as many as you can think of).
- If I had to pick the top three skills, which would they be?
- Do I possess these skills and if so, are they at the level they need to be?
- Which one skill would have the most impact and make the most difference? (Start with that one)

H – Habits

- What routines would help me make consistent progress?
- Which habits or routines will help with skill development, knowledge or building relationships?
- What is the first habit I need to develop? (Start making this a daily habit by making it a mini-habit)
- Are there bad habits negatively impacting my success? If so, look for the cues that trigger them and find new habits to replace them with.

R – Relationships

- Who has done/ is doing what I want to accomplish?
- Where can I find /connect with other like-minded people?
- Is there someone in my life that is having an adverse influence on me?
- What are the top three relationships that are specific to helping me reach my goal?
- Who is the first person I should connect with?

K – Knowledge

- What specific information do I need to learn about my goal?
- What is the minimum amount that I need to know to get started?
- What are the best resources to gain this knowledge?

As you begin to complete the map, you will have a very clear picture of your plan and the next step you need to take. If you're not sure how to answer any of the questions above, then perhaps you need more information on what it takes to accomplish your goal. As I've stated before, if you're not sure where to start, then the first step is to connect with someone that has already accomplished what you want to do and learn from them. Find out how they did it, what knowledge they needed and which skills they had. What kind of relationships did they build and what are their beliefs?

Beliefs – These questions are designed to help you get more familiar with yourself and are only just a sample. You should have enough to get started if you answered the previous questions but the following are incredibly important and should be an ongoing review process.

- What is my philosophy or beliefs about success?
- Do I believe achieving my goal is possible?
- Have I set false expectations?
- Why do I want to accomplish this goal?
- Do I believe I am worthy of this accomplishment?
- Are there limiting beliefs holding me back?
- Which empowering beliefs would help me the most?

Track It! - The Victory Calendar

Now that you have a simple outline on how to begin applying each of the six elements, your next step is to start taking action. When it comes to taking action, it's important that you track and measure your progress so you can make adjustments as needed. One of my favorite tools is The Victory Calendar and it's also highly motivational and great for keeping momentum. It takes very little time to maintain but quickly begins to give you positive feedback on your progress. The Victory Calendar is simply a visual representation of the days you have taken action toward one of the six elements.

Here is how it works: Start with any calendar that has a spot for you to add a note to each day. This could be a physical calendar on your wall, a daily journal or a simple phone app. Next, for each day that you take action toward one of the six elements, you add the letter that represents that respective component. For example, if I worked on a new Habit today, then I would put an 'H' for today. If I read my goals this morning, I would put an 'A.' Some of these will overlap so you can get credit for multiple elements by taking a single action.

Even after just one week, you will begin to see a visual trend on how many days you are winning (i.e. taking action) versus how many days were lost (you did nothing). The goal is to never have a blank day. Even if you cannot act on multiple elements, you should at a minimum have at least one letter down for each day. The reason for this is psychological. Even the tiniest actions will begin to create momentum when done consistently over a longer period of time. It's highly motivational to look back at a monthly calendar that is covered in S's, H's, A's, R's, K's and B's! Sometimes it can feel like you're not making progress but a quick look at The Victory Calendar will remind you how much you've actually done.

It will soon become a game and the longer your winning streak goes, the more likely you are to continue it. Once you have a series of weeks or months with consistent progress toward a habit or skill, you will be more inclined to take action on those days that you feel tired, discouraged or just lazy. You wouldn't dare of leaving a blank day! Time flies and the days quickly become weeks and your weeks soon turn into months and years. It's easy to forget or put off your actions and goals for another day so the Victory Calendar also serves as a way to keep you accountable to yourself. Remember, success doesn't happen overnight and consistent action over time will suddenly begin to yield massive results as the compounding effect starts to take hold.

Follow the 90/10 rule to give yourself the greatest shot at success. Achieving goals in life requires both planning and strategizing as well as effective execution. However, the ratio between these two must be 90/10. That means for every hour you spend planning, you need to spend nine hours working toward your goal. Most people get this backwards and they spend incredible amounts of time planning, dreaming and talking about their goal while investing very little time on the actual grind. For example, if you're building a new business, don't spend countless hours designing a beautiful business card and logo. Instead, use all that energy to get a prototype of your product or service made and get out into the market place to test it. Go out there and talk to prospective customers, get feedback and build some momentum. Sure, it's fun and exciting to dream about what your business could look like in a few years but there real value is in the actual work. Whatever your goal, if you stick to the 90/10 rule, you'll find yourself making consistent progress and you'll always achieve your goals faster.

"Accept the challenges so that you can feel the exhilaration of victory!"
— *General George S. Patton*

CHAPTER TEN

SHARK Belief Your Life!

Over 15 years ago, I embarked on a quest to find the formula for success. I believed that there were common traits among those who succeed and I was determined to discover what they were. Although it took me just a few months to write this book, it's actually the product of years of study and experience, reading hundreds of books, and listening to thousands of hours of audio. I've invested a lot of money and time on seminars, classes, and training. It was my personal successes as well as my failures that motivated me to identify the six core elements. This is the book I wish I had been given all those years ago. Even then, the discoveries I made were only possible because of the many that came before me; those who had dedicated a lifetime to studying and sharing the philosophies of success. Notables such as Napoleon Hill, Jim Rohn, Les Brown, and Tony Robbins to name just a few. It is the many teachers and advisors that I owe credit to and just as I started this book, I will repeat once again, "If I have seen further, it is by standing on the shoulders of Giants."

I continue to dedicate myself to learning and improving, but I'm also confident that the simple approach I've presented hold the keys for anyone who wants to achieve great things with their life. Achieving excellence is not the byproduct of luck or talent. A life of excellence is chosen and pursued. You have the power to choose your own goals, the power to take action towards them and ultimately, the power to change the trajectory of your life. Some will say that SHARK Belief is too complicated and still others will claim that it's too simple. I ask that you first put forth an honest attempt at applying the six elements by using the methods I've described before you make your final conclusion on the merits of this approach.

Is Success Guaranteed?

People often ask me if I guarantee that they will be successful if they begin using the SHARK Belief Success Code. That's difficult to answer because of the countless variables within each of our lives, but I will attempt to provide some clarity with the following illustration. Every farmer understands there are some minimum requirements for growing a crop. If a farmer wants to succeed, several vital elements are required regardless of the type of crop. This includes things such as planting seeds, fertile soil, water, and sunlight. Seeds are essential if one is to grow a crop, but the act of planting a seed does not guarantee that a crop will grow. Likewise, once the plants have sprouted they must receive water, but just because the plants are watered does not guarantee that they will yield a harvest. Many external variables could influence the yield, and there are a number of risks that could prevent a successful crop.

You see, just like growing a crop, some necessary elements must be in place before you can succeed, but just because these elements are there does not mean that success will automatically be the end result. The reality is that most people fail, not because they didn't have the right skills or know the right people, but people fail simply because they didn't work hard enough or persist long enough. It often comes down to just that; you have to execute and you have persevere. Many claim they worked hard, but looking back it's evident that they didn't make the necessary sacrifices. Too much time was wasted on procrastination, watching videos or taking the weekends off. If you really want to make something happen, it's going to take more than working from 9 to 5. I promise there will be some late nights and long weekends. It's going to take more than working five days a week. It will cost you. The question is how bad do you want it and are you willing to do what's necessary? Are you willing to make the necessary sacrifices? You may have to give up some temporary comforts. You'll need to delay instant gratification and hustle, even on those days when you'd rather just sleep in and watch movies. That is the only way to give yourself the best shot at success.

The goal is to do everything within your power to yield success, and that means starting with all the essential ingredients. However, even if you employ all six elements, diligently work hard and believe with all your heart, there is still the possibility that you will not succeed. That's just reality. Some industries are ultra-competitive and the margins for victory are incredibly narrow. Other times, you just pick the wrong industry, the wrong product, or the wrong time. Just know that while you must give it your all and employ the six elements in the SHARK Belief Success Code, it's impossible to eliminate all risk. Some setbacks are the result of things outside of your control. There are very little guarantees in life and if

191

you're waiting for one before you get started, I'm afraid you'll never achieve the success you want.

"You miss 100 percent of the shots you never take."

- Wayne Gretzky

SHARK Belief Your Life!

You now have the code that can help you succeed at anything. The rest is up to you. You must begin to take action. Use this book as a guide and come back to it often. We often need to review something several times before we begin to actually understand it. I implore you to dedicate yourself to truly understanding the SHARK Belief Success Code and making it a part of your everyday life. Once you begin to see SHARK Belief work for you, you will start to see that it can go far beyond the goals you've set for yourself. You will begin to approach most areas of your life with this mindset. As I stated at the beginning, it's more than a formula or a process. It becomes a way of life.

They say the best way to learn something is to teach it to someone else. Share what you've learned here with someone else and teach them the elements necessary for success in their own lives. My vision is to see one million people learn and use this approach, and that can only be done with the help of others. We will see incredible changes in our world when SHARK Belief becomes a way of life. Instead of stumbling for years trying to learn the path to success, we'll see others starting off on the right track and using their energy to focus on the goals in front of them. They will get there much more efficiently and in a shorter time. They will be able to accomplish bigger goals and see great success. Much like science and technology have advanced further from the knowledge and discoveries that have come before them, SHARK Belief has built a foundation from which others can build.

Life is about progress and advancing mankind for the better. It's the beauty of education and innovation. We often see this in technology. Just look at how long it took for what are now basic concepts such as algebra and calculus to be discovered. It took thousands of years and was the realm of only the brightest scientific minds of the day. Now, we expect our high school students to master these concepts before graduation so they can move on to bigger and more complex things. It's not that we have become smarter or superior to our ancestors, it's just that our techniques have improved and we are building upon the knowledge and understanding that has been passed down to us. We see this same phenomenon in every field from sports to medicine to communications technology. Why not do the same for the area of business, personal development, and success? That was the purpose for me writing this book. You now have the blueprint you need to accomplish greater things in your life.

Success is within your reach and is entirely possible for you. The groundwork has been laid for you and you can now approach your goals much more effectively and see results much sooner. There is no need for you to start from the bottom. Commit to a life of personal development and growth and you will always end with satisfaction and fulfillment. Success is not about your possessions or the accolades you receive. The rewards of excellence come from the person you become. Life has given you two beautiful gifts: your mind and your time. Don't waste time or mental energy on frivolous pursuits. Use your time to become the person you were meant to be. Enlarge your thinking, grow and make progress. Make the most of every day. While learning the principles taught here, you likely had a goal in mind or were reminded of a dream you've had. You now have the formula that will give you the greatest shot at realizing it. Become that person who lives the life you've always dreamed of. SHARK Belief your life!

BIBLIOGRAPHY

Adler, Mortimer, and Van Doren, Charles. *How to Read a Book.* Touchstone 1972.

Allen, James. *As a Man Thinketh.* New York: J P Tarcher/Penguin, 2008.

Branson, Richard. *Losing My Virginity.* New York: Crown Business, 2011.

Byrne, Rhonda. *The Secret.* New York: Atria, 2006.

Cardone, Grant. *The 10x Rule.* Hoboken, NJ: John Wiley & Sons, 2011.

Carnegie, Dale. *How to Win Friends & Influence People.* New York: Pocket, 1998.

Colvin, Geoffrey. *Talent Is Overrated.* New York: Portfolio, 2010.

Coyle, Daniel. *The Talent Code.* New York: Bantam, 2009.

Duhigg, Charles. *The Power of Habit.* New York: Random House, 2012.

Elrod, Hal. The Miracle Morning. 2012

Ferrazzi, Keith, and Tahl Raz. *Never Eat Alone.* Crown Business, 2014.

Ferriss, Timothy. *The 4-hour Chef.* Boston: New Harvest, 2012.

Ferriss, Timothy. *The 4-hour Work Week.* Chatham: Vermilion, 2011.

Foer, Joshua. *Moonwalking with Einstein.* New York: Penguin, 2011.

Gladwell, Malcolm. *Outliers*. New York: Little Brown, 2008.

Guise, Stephen. *Mini Habits*. 2013.

Hill, Napoleon. *The Think & Grow Rich*. New York: Plume, 1988.

Hill, Napoleon. *The Law of Success: Original 1925 Edition*. Beverly, MA: Orne, 2010.

Kaufman, Josh. *The First 20 Hours*. Portfolio 2014.

Kiyosaki, Robert T., and Sharon L. Lechter. *Rich Dad, Poor Dad*. New York: Warner Business, 2000.

Luttrell, Marcus, and Patrick Robinson. *Lone Survivor*. Little Brown and Company 2007.

Maltz, Maxwell. *Psycho-cybernetics*. New York: Pocket, 1969.

Mandino, Og. *The Greatest Salesman in the World*. New York: Bantam, 1991.

McCormack, Mark H. What They Don't Teach You at Harvard Business School. Toronto: Bantam, 1984.

Newport, Cal. *So Good They Can't Ignore You*. New York: Business Plus, 2012.

Nightingale, Earl. *The Strangest Secret*. United States: BN Pub., 2006.

Robbins, Anthony. *Awaken the Giant Within*. New York, NY: Summit, 1991.

Schwartz, David Joseph. *The Magic of Thinking Big*. New York: Simon & Schuster, 1987.

Schwarzenegger, Arnold, and Peter Petre. *Total Recall*. Simon & Schuster, 2013.

Siebold, Steve. *How Rich People Think*. London House, 2010.

Small, Gary. *The Memory Bible*. New York: Hyperion, 2002.

Syed, Matthew. *Bounce*. New York: Perennial, 2011.

Tracy, Brian. Change Your Thinking, Change Your Life. Wiley 2005.

Vance, Ashlee. *Elon Musk*. Ecco, 2015.

Made in the USA
San Bernardino, CA
04 March 2016